A Rational Classification of Literature

FOR

SHELVING AND CATALOGUING BOOKS.

This classification is published in consequence of a year's practice with Mr. Dewey's "Decimal System."

1. This system, and indeed any system, of classification may be used with either the movable or the fixed location. The chief difference is, that if the movable system is used, the books can be shelved in one unbroken row to begin with, and then shifted along as new books are inserted at their proper points in the line; while on the fixed system the space disposable for books needs to be mapped out to begin with, so that the row of books on each subject shall begin at the point where it is to remain. But Mr. Dewey's system (for example) could be used in the fixed-location manner, by simply mapping out the whole space of the shelves as before, beginning the row of books on each separate subject at a given place, and then keeping them there.

In both systems (as commonly used, *but not necessarily*) books newly added are placed at the ends of sections; i. e., books on Archæology, at the end of the row of books on that subject already shelved; books on Spectroscopy at the end of the row of books on Spectroscopy already shelved, etc.

The numbering of the books in the two systems must, of course, differ: in the movable system it expresses the place of the book *in the classification only;* and in the fixed system, the place on the shelf, and in the classification too.

2. The classifying on the shelf need not be more than an approximate one, in most libraries. In specialty libraries, particularly where readers may go to the shelves and work in the alcoves (as in college libraries chiefly for the instructors), it may be a convenience to have all the books on each subject accurately together. Usually, however, a rough approximation will do very well; the indispensable condition being, not the scientific accuracy of the location of the book, but mechanical accuracy of its place on the shelf, exactly where its shelf-mark situates it, so as to be readily found when wanted. Any closer classification can be provided in the catalogue.

3. The classification here offered wholly neglects decimalism, and seeks to give to each subject just as many subdivisions as it requires. Under "Europe,"

for instance, it allows, not ten countries, but as many countries, divisions, etc. as there are.

It is in no sense founded on Mr. Dewey's system, its substance having been in print (reference alphabet and all) long before that very ingenious and symmetrical device was worked out by its enterprising and energetic author.

4. Criticisms on Mr. Dewey's system are unnecessary here. Those who like it will naturally adhere to it. The writer believes that his system accomplishes some good things which Mr. Dewey's does not, and cures some defects in it. Probably Mr. Dewey may reciprocate these sentiments.

5. Points (among others) of the present system:

First. THREEFOLD ANALYSIS.—Literature is laid off into eight classes, these into seventy chapters, and these again into a little more than 1,400 sections, with blanks left which will allow of expansion to 6,384 or more sections. The class names and the chapter names are used as labels or guides only, and have no number in the series of topics. It is the sections or ultimate subdivisions alone that have such numbers; and under these heads are to be placed the titles of the works in the library. The names of these sections are meant to be suitable for subject-heads in a catalogue; so that, in fact, each section name, along with its group of titles of single works, might safely be transferred to its alphabetical place in what is often called a "dictionary" catalogue. One change would, however, be necessary: the books are placed on the shelf at the end of each section in the order of their coming into the library; while in the catalogue they should be entered under the name of the section in the alphabetical order of the names of authors.

Second. EXPANSIBILITY.—Numbers are cheap, and just as many have been taken as was found convenient. For instance, after section 4 is this entry: "5–504, 500 blanks for alphabeting languages." Now in any small or moderately large general library, the single section 4, next before this supply of blanks (i. e., "Versions in other languages") will be ample for all such versions of the Bible in the library, as they will altogether cover but little space on the shelf. But in a large library, especially if its biblical department is full, the German Bibles (for instance) will form quite a series; the Latin ones another; and so on. Such blank numbers have been provided at those points in the series where further subdivision seemed most likely to be required.

A similar case will be found under Portuguese, Italian, and German languages (4970, 4978, 4986), where blank numbers are left for subdividing as fully as under English, should it be convenient.

Further subdivisions can be made at any point, by adding a letter to the figure (as 4994 A, 4994 B, etc.); or by Mr. Dewey's device of adding another digit (as, 49940, 49941, etc.); and there are other methods.

Third. NATURALNESS —The divisions and subdivisions of subjects are meant to coincide with facts, so that each book shall fall into its right place with as little reasoning as possible.

Fourth. VARIABILITY.—In using this system in a small library, the eight

A Rational Classification of Literature for Shelving and Cataloguing Books in a Library

Frederic Beecher Perkins

Copyright © BiblioLife, LLC

This historical reproduction is part of a unique project that provides opportunities for readers, educators and researchers by bringing hard-to-find original publications back into print at reasonable prices. Because this and other works are culturally important, we have made them available as part of our commitment to protecting, preserving and promoting the world's literature. These books are in the "public domain" and were digitized and made available in cooperation with libraries, archives, and open source initiatives around the world dedicated to this important mission.

We believe that when we undertake the difficult task of re-creating these works as attractive, readable and affordable books, we further the goal of sharing these works with a global audience, and preserving a vanishing wealth of human knowledge.

Many historical books were originally published in small fonts, which can make them very difficult to read. Accordingly, in order to improve the reading experience of these books, we have created "enlarged print" versions of our books. Because of font size variation in the original books, some of these may not technically qualify as "large print" books, as that term is generally defined; however, we believe these versions provide an overall improved reading experience for many.

RATIONAL CLASSIFICATION

OF

LITERATURE

FOR

SHELVING AND CATALOGUING BOOKS

IN A

LIBRARY.

WITH ALPHABETICAL INDEX.

BY

FRED. B. PERKINS.

SAN FRANCISCO:
BACON & COMPANY, BOOK AND JOB PRINTERS,
Corner Clay and Sansome Streets.
1881.

classes above might be the only divisions employed, each to have its number, from 1 to 8. In a larger library the chapters might be employed, which would give a series of seventy divisions; and it is believed that the system at full length might be used in any library, no matter how large.

Indeed, this classification, with its alphabetical key index, admits of many changes. Thus, the section numbers might be made to skip one throughout (i.e., by running 1, 3, 5, etc., instead of 1, 2, 3, etc.), or to skip four, by running 1, 5, 10, etc., thus giving room for much greater subdivision; or these expansions might be applied to any single chapter or class. New figures would probably be needed for all the subsequent portions of the classification, and the corresponding changes should of course be made in the index.

Fifth. CROSS REFERENCES.—It is believed that the (not very numerous) cross references which have been introduced will be useful as guides in an occasional doubt how to classify a new book, or how to pursue some research. They might, with the necessary changes of form, be advantageously transferred, along with the heads under which they stand, to a catalogue.

Sixth. CLASSIFICATION BY CONTRADICTORIES.—This method has been applied only in a few cases, and it might probably have been more extensively used with advantage. Many readers would be helped by finding the books on each side of a debated question indicated separately. Such cases are, Woman Suffrage, *for*, and Woman Suffrage, *against;* Capital Punishment, and *Same, works against;* and the like. It can, however, be easily introduced anywhere, by inserting the necessary additional section.

6. In regard to History, Geography, and Travels, a choice was made between these systems, namely:

a. To make three separate classes of them, or two such classes (by putting Geography and Travels together), in which event many countries would appear in three or two separate places; the classification for Geography and for Travels being substantially identical with that for History.

b. To deal with each country, continent, etc., only once for all three, subclassifying where necessary. This is what has been done, as on the whole the more convenient of the two.

In Biography, the double classification (i. e., applied to both collective and individual biographies) employed is believed an improvement. All the individual biography can at any time be thrown into a single alphabet, if desired for cataloguing purposes, by author's names, or (which is much the more convenient way) by names of subjects or (to coin a word) *biographees.*

Two chapter-heads have been inserted as convenient ones, for which better names would be welcome. These are "Historical Collaterals" (including 1769-1872) and "Linguistics" (5531-53). No more satisfactory description was found for the collection of subjects placed under the former, and the latter has been used without leave, as a label for the formal methods of expressing and recording thought by language; "Philology" being taken for the science of language.

THE CLASSES AND CHAPTERS.

CLASS A.—RELIGION.
CHAP.
  I. BIBLE, BIBLICAL STUDY.
  II. HISTORY OF RELIGION.
  III. SYSTEMATIC THEOLOGY.
  IV. CHRISTIAN POLITY.
  V. DEVOTIONAL.
  VI. PRACTICAL.
  VII. COLLECTIVE WORKS.

B.—PHILOSOPHY.
  I. MENTAL PHILOSOPHY: HISTORY AND SYSTEMS.
  II. MENTAL PHILOSOPHY: DEPARTMENTS.
  III. MIND AND BODY.
  IV. MORAL PHILOSOPHY.

C.—SOCIETY.
  I. GOVERNMENT AND LAW.
  II. PUBLIC ADMINISTRATION.
  III. SOCIAL ORGANIZATION.
  IV. POLITICAL ECONOMY.
  V. EDUCATION: METHODS AND DEPARTMENTS.
  VI. EDUCATION: INSTITUTIONS AND REPORTS.
  VII. BUSINESS.

D.—HISTORY.
  I. GENERAL GEOGRAPHY AND TRAVELS.
  II. UNIVERSAL HISTORY.
  III. HISTORICAL COLLATERALS.
  IV. ANCIENT HISTORY.
  V. MEDIEVAL HISTORY.
  VI. MODERN AND EUROPEAN HISTORY.
  VII. ASIA.
  VIII. AFRICA.
  IX. SOUTH SEAS, AUSTRALASIA, SINGLE ISLANDS.
  X. AMERICA, EXCEPT UNITED STATES.
  XI. UNITED STATES.

E.—BIOGRAPHY.
  I. COLLECTIVE: GENERALLY AND BY NATIONS.
  II. BY CLASSES.
  III. GENEALOGY AND NAMES.

F.—SCIENCE.
  I. GENERAL TREATISES.
  II. MATHEMATICS.
  III. NATURAL PHILOSOPHY.
  IV. ASTRONOMY.
  V. COSMOLOGY.
  VI. GEOLOGY.
  VII. CHEMISTRY.
  VIII. GENERAL NATURAL HISTORY AND ZOOLOGY.
  IX. BOTANY.
  X. GENERAL MEDICINE.
  XI. HYGIENE.
  XII. MEDICAL PRACTICE.
  XIII. SURGICAL PRACTICE.
  XIV. MEDICAL JURISPRUDENCE.

G.—ARTS.
  I. GENERAL TREATISES.
  II. ENGINEERING.
  III. ARCHITECTURE.
  IV. MILITARY ARTS.
  V. NAVAL ARTS.
  VI. MECHANIC ARTS AND TRADES.
  VII. AGRICULTURE.
  VIII. DOMESTIC ARTS.
  IX. FINE ARTS.
  X. MUSIC.
  XI. RECREATIONS.

H.—LITERATURE.
  I. HISTORY OF LITERATURE.
  II. PHILOLOGY.
  III. LINGUISTICS.
  IV. CRITICAL SCIENCE.
  V. POETRY.
  VI. DRAMA.
  VII. FICTION.
  VIII. ORATORY.
  IX. COLLECTIONS.
  X. PERIODICALS.
  XI. ENCYCLOPEDIAS.
  XII. BIBLIOGRAPHY.
  XIII. LIBRARIES.

CLASSES, CHAPTERS AND SECTIONS.

NOTE.—The sections numbered in one series of Arabic figures, running through the whole classification, are the names of the topics or subjects under which the books are to be arranged on the shelves, and also in the topical part of the catalogue.

CLASS A.—RELIGION

Chapter I. Bible, biblical study.

For other sacred books, see names of religions in Chapter II.
Inspiration of Bible, 867, 868.
Bible societies, 937.
Hebrew language, 4713.

Section.
1. Bible, texts: polyglots.
2.   originals alone.
3.   English versions.
4.   versions in other languages.
5–504. *Blanks for alphabeting languages.*
505. Old Testament, texts.
506. New Testament, texts.
507. Other parts of Bible.
508. Harmonies of the Gospels.
509. Apocrypha, commonly so called.
510. Other apocryphal books; Old Testament; Judaic.
511.   New Testament; Christian.
512. Canon of Scripture.
513. Commentaries: whole Bible.
514.   Old Testament and parts.
515.   New Testament and parts.
516–83. single books of Bible.
584. Hermeneutics.
585. Biblical encyclopedias and dictionaries.
586. History of Bible.
587. Biblical antiquities.
588. Biblical Geography. *See also* Palestine, 2103.
589. Biblical natural history.
590. Concordances.
591–610. Other biblical aids.

II. History of Religion.

Symbolism, 1832.
Christian art, 4291.
Mythology, 1807 etc.
611. History of religion generally.
612. History of Christianity.
For history of other religions and of sects, see their names below. For history of doctrines, see names of sects, and also, under Chapter III., Systematic Theology.
613. Persecution; toleration.
614. Apostolic and primitive church.
615. Patristics.
616. Greek and eastern churches.
617. Monachism generally.
618. Church of Rome: history.
619.   theology. *Canon law,* 1238.
620.   monachism in.
621.   Jesuits.
622.   Inquisition.
Missions, 934.
623.   works against.
624. Modern church history generally.
625. Albigenses, Waldenses, Vaudois.
626. Protestantism generally.
627. Reformation.
628. Lutheranism.
629. Calvinism.
630. Church of England.
631. English dissent generally.
632. Puritanism.
633. Puseyism; ritualism.
634. Scottish Episcopal church.

635	Scottish kirk.	856	Philosophy of religion. *Religion and Philosophy*, 864.
636	Episcopal church in U. S.	857	Supernaturalism.
637	Presbyterians.	858	Atheist works.
638	Congregationalists and Independents.	859	Works against atheism.
639	Methodists; Arminianism.	860	Deist, infidel, rationalist works.
640	Baptists. *Baptism*, 929, 930.	861	Works against deism, infidelity, rationalism.
641	Reformed (Dutch) church.	862	Pantheist works.
642	Moravians.	863	Works against pantheism.
643	Quakers.	864	Religion and philosophy.
644	Unitarians.		See also Inspiration of Bible, against, 868.
	God, trinitarianism, 873, 874.		See also Miracles, against, 862.
	Christ, 875, 876.		See also Prophecy, against, 870.
	atonement, 877.	865	Religion and science.
645	Universalists.	866	Evidences of Christianity.
	eschatology, 882.	867	Inspiration of the Bible.
	future state, 855.	868	works against.
	hell, 887.	869	Prophecy.
	devil, 886.	870	works against truth of.
646–700	Other Christian sects.	871	Miracles.
701	Christian mysticism.	872	works against truth of.
702	Swedenborgianism.	873	God: Trinitarian works.
703	Shakers.	874	anti-trinitarian works.
704	Mormons. *Utah,* 2388.		See also Unitarianism, 644.
705	Judaism. *Jews, ancient,* 1897; *medieval and modern,* 1958.	875	Christ.
		876	works against deity and divinity of.
706	Mohammedanism.		See also Unitarians, 644.
707	Brahmanism.	877	Atonement, salvation; grace; redemption.
708	Jainism.	878	Holy Ghost; regeneration; sanctification.
709	Sikh religion.	879	Depravity.
710	Buddhism.	880	Freewill; predestination; fatalism.
711	Confucianism.	881	Faith; justification.
712	Taouism.	882	Eschatology generally.
713–15	Other Chinese beliefs.	883	Millennium; second advent.
716	Sintooism.	884	Death; resurrection.
717	Zoroastrianism and Parsism.	885	Future state; immortality.
718–817	Heathenism, other and generally.	886	Angels, devil, devils.
818	Spiritism.	887	Hell; eternal punishment.
819	Witchcraft, sorcery, magic, divination.	888–920	Other single doctrines.
820–50	Religious superstitions, fanaticisms, and extravagances, other and generally.		

III. Systematic Theology.

For theologies of sects and religions see their names in Chapter II.
Theological schools, 1596.

851 Theological encyclopedias and dictionaries.
852 History of doctrines generally.
853 History of heresies.
854 Creeds.
855 Natural theology.

IV. Christian Polity.

Church architecture and ecclesiology, 3581.
Church and schools, 1520.
Theological schools, 1596.

921 Church polity generally.
922 Ecclesiastical law.
   Canon law, 1328.
923 Ecclesiastical trials.
924 Church and state.
   Persecution, 613.

925	Rites and ceremonies.		**VI. Practical.**
	Prayer-books, service-books, liturgies, 962.	965	Conversion; revivals.
926	Ordinances generally.	966	Christian life.
927	Sabbath, Sabbath reform, Sunday laws.	967	Christian ethics.
928	Lord's supper.	968	Religious fiction and allegory.
929	Baptism; Baptist views.	969	Religious anecdotes.
930	Anti-Baptist views.	970–90	Other practical topics.
931	Pastoral theology.		
932	Homiletics.		**VII. Collective Works.**
	Sermons, 994.		*Collective biographies of Christians and of clergy,* 2507–10.
	Rhetoric, 5537.	991	Religious encyclopedias.
	Elocution, 5536.		*For those on the Bible and biblical topics exclusively, see* 585; *on theology,* 851.
933	Missions generally.	992	Religious periodicals.
	Biographies of Missionaries, 2509–10.		*For those devoted to particular sects or subjects, see also under names of such.*
934	Romanist.	993	Collections of works; complete works.
935	Protestant, foreign.		*For those devoted to particular sects or subjects, see under names of such.*
936	Protestant, home.	994	Collections of sermons.
937	Bible societies.		*For such collections, or for single sermons, on a single subject, see under its name.*
938	Tract societies.	995	Occasional sermons.
939	Sunday schools.		*For obituary and historical discourses, see under names of their subjects, in Biography and History.*
940	Religious charities generally.	996	Collections of religious essays.
941	Young Men's Christian Associations and Unions.		*For such collections, or for single essays, on one subject, see its name*
942–60	Other religious institutions.	997–1000	*blank.*
	V. Devotional.		
961	Prayer.		
962	Prayer-books, liturgies, service-books.		
963	Meditations.		
964	Hymnology		

CLASS B.—PHILOSOPHY.

	I. History of Mental Philosophy.	1043	Epicureans.
		1044	Stoics.
	Biographies of philosophers. 2525–6	1045	Alexandrians.
1001	Encyclopedias and dictionaries.	1046–70	Other ancient.
1002	Periodicals and transactions.	1071	Patristic.
1003	Histories of mental philosophy generally.	1072	Scholastic.
1004	of ancient philosophy generally.	1073–1100	*blank.*
1005	oriental philosophy generally.	1101	Arabian.
1006–35	*blank.*	1102	Modern generally.
1036	Greek and Roman philosophy generally.	1103	Descartes and school.
1037	early Greek philosophy generally.	1104	Spinoza.
1038	Sophists, Socrates.	1105	Locke.
1039	Plato.	1106	Hume.
1040	Aristotle.	1107	Scotch.
1041	Pyrrhonists.	1108	Wolff.
1042	Neo-Platonists.	1109	Kant.

1110	Hegel.	1277	Mind and body generally.
1111	Fichte	1278	Phrenology.
1112	Schelling.	1279	books against.
1113	Cousin: Eclecticism.	1280	Temperaments.
1114	Other French.	1281	Physiognomy.
1115	Positivism.	1282	Sleep, dreams, somnambulism.
1116	Pessimism.	1283	Animal magnetism.
1117	Recent English.	1284	Delusions, hallucinations.
1118	American.		
1119–1200	Other.		

For religious ones, see 819, etc.
Insanity, 3279.

II. Departments of Mental Philosophy.

For philosophies of separate subjects, see under their names, as, Philosophy of religion, 856, etc.
Religion and philosophy, 864.

1201 Methodology.
1202 Classification of knowledge.
1203 Logic.
1204–20 *blank.*
1221 Metaphysics generally,
1222 Ontology.
1223 Biology.
1224 Psychology.
1225–75 Individual faculties.
1276 Hermetics.

III. Mind and Body.

For medical works, see under Medicine.
Anthropology, 2823.

IV. Moral Philosophy.

Christian ethics, 967.
Medical ethics, 3523.
Slavery, 1463–5.

1285 History of ethics.
1286 Systems of ethics.
1287 Formation of character.
   Christian life, 966
   Self-education, 1514.
1288 Morals of politics.
1289   amusements.
1290   stimulants and narcotics.
1291   business.
1292   marriage.
1293 Morals for young men.
1294   young women.
1295 Morals of social intercourse.
   Etiquette, 1838.
1296–1320 Other applications of ethics.

CLASS C.—SOCIETY.

I. Law.

Law schools, 1594.
Parliamentary law, 1401.
Medical jurisprudence, 3521.
Biography of lawyers and judges, 2519, 2520.

1321 Law dictionaries.
1322 Periodicals.
1323 Histories.
1324 General treatises.
1325 International law; diplomacy; treaties.
1326 Ancient law generally.
1327 Roman and civil law.
1328 Canon law.
1329 Constitutional law generally.
1330   English.
1331   United States.
1332   French.
1333–52 Other.
1353 Common law generally.
1354 Real property; wills.
1355 Commercial law.
1356 Maritime law.
1357 Criminal law.
   Crimes and punishments, 1413.
   Capital punishment, 1414–15.
   Juvenile criminals, 1412.
   Criminal reform, 1411.
1358 Military law, courts-martial.
1359 Law of evidence.
1360 Codes.
1361 Statutes.
1362 Digests.

1363 Pleading and procedure.
1364 Forms and precedents.
1365 Criminal trials. *Lives of criminals,* 2511, 2512.
1366 Civil trials.
Ecclesiastical law, 922.
Ecclesiastical trials, 923.
1367 Patent law. *Inventions, patents,* 3809.
1368 Copyright law.
1369–94 Other branches of law.

II. Public Administration.

Church polity, 921.
Church and state, 924.
Sunday laws, 927.
Morals of politics, 1288.
Biographies of statesmen, 2539–40.

1395 Government generally.
1396 Republicanism.
1397 Elective franchise.
1398 Woman suffrage; for.
1399   against.
1400 Legislation and administration generally.
1401 Parliamentary law.
1402 Police.
1403 Fire departments.
1404 Postal administration.
1405 Public health generally.
Hospitals and dispensaries, 3271.
1406 Prostitution.
medically, 3278.
1407 Parks and public gardens.
1408 Burial, cemeteries, cremation.
1409 Public charities generally.
Blind asylums, 1604.
Deaf and dumb asylums, 1603.
Idiot schools, 1605.
Lunatic asylums, 3279.
Religious charities, 940.
1410 Pauperism; poor laws.
1411 Reform and correctional institutions.
1412 Juvenile criminals.
Reform schools, 1607.
1413 Crimes and punishments.
1414 Capital punishment.
1415   Works against.
1416 Registration and census methods.
For census volumes see names of countries.
1417–32 Other administrative departments.
1433 Civil service reform.

III. Social Organization.

History of civilization, 1767.
Prehistoric archæology, 1772.
Domestic arts, 4253–80.
Lives of reformers and benefactors, 2531, 2532.

1434 Periodicals and transactions.
1435 General treatises.
1436 Socialism.
1437 Communism.
1438 Women's rights.
Female education, 1511–12.
Woman suffrage, 1398, 1399.
1439 Marriage and divorce.
Marriage customs, 1839.
Morals of marriage, 1292.
1440 Secret societies generally.
1441 Freemasonry.
1442 Odd Fellows.
1443–58 Other secret organizations.
1459 Peace reform.
1460 Immigration; naturalization.
1461 Colonial systems.
British colonial history, 1995; *and see names of separate colonies.*
United States, colonial period, 2330.
1462 African colonization.
1463 Slavery generally.
1464 England and slavery.
1465 American slavery and abolition.

IV. Political Economy.

Statistics, 1770.

1466 General treatises.
1467 Public finance.
Money and currency, 1688.
1468 Protectionist works.
1469 Free-trade works.
1470 Capital and labor; wages question.
1471 Co-operative systems.
1472 Trade unions, guilds.
1473 Strikes.
1474 Building associations.
1475 Savings banks; friendly societies.
1476–1500 Other topics in political economy.

V. Education: Methods and Departments.

Biographies of educators and teachers, 2517–18.

1501 Encyclopedias.

1502	Periodicals and transactions.	1595	Medical schools.
1503	Histories.	1596	Theological schools.
1504	General treatises.	1597	Scientific schools.
1505	Public education generally.	1598	Technological schools.
1506	American.	1599	Military and naval schools.
1507	Foreign.	1600	Business colleges.
1508	Special education generally.	1601	Normal schools.
1509	Classical education.	1602	Industrial and manual-labor schools.
1510	Scientific education.	1603	Deaf and dumb asylums.
1511	Female education.	1604	Blind asylums.
1512	Art education.	1605	Idiot schools.
	Musical education, 4467, 4473.	1606	Ragged schools.
1513	Co-education of sexes.	1607	Reform schools.
1514	Home education.		*Juvenile criminals,* 1412.
1515	Self education.	1608–27	*blank.*
1516	Courses of reading; reading clubs.		
1517	Debating societies.		**VII. Business.**
1518	Adult education.		
1519	Education of teachers.		*Morals of business,* 1291.
1520	Church and schools.		*Public finance,* 1467.
1521	Systems of instruction generally.		*Commercial law,* 1355.
1522–53	by subjects, singly.		*Arts and trades, class G.*
1554	School algebras.		*Business colleges,* 1600.
1555	arithmetics.		*Biography of business men,* 2505–6.
1556	geographies.	1628	Commercial dictionaries.
1557	histories.	1629	Periodicals and transactions.
1558	readers.	1630	History of commerce and trade generally.
1559	spellers.	1631	of United States.
1560	writing-books.	1632	of other countries.
1561	Other school-books.	1633	Transportation.
1562	School architecture.	1634	Corporations generally.
1563	School furniture and fittings.	1635	Mining corporations.
1564	School apparatus, philosophical.	1636	Railroad corporations.
1565–84	*blank.*	1637–86	Other corporations.
		1687	Banks and banking.
	VI. Education: Institutions and Reports.		*Savings banks,* 1475.
		1688	Money and currency.
1585	Public schools.	1689	Stocks, exchange, investments.
1586	Private schools.	1690	Weights and measures.
1587	Primary schools.	1691	Metric system.
1588	Kindergarten.	1692	Insurance generally.
1589	Secondary schools.	1693	life.
1590	High and grammar schools.	1694	fire and marine.
1591	Classical schools.	1695	Book-keeping.
1592	Colleges and universities.	1696	Mercantile manuals, forms, tables.
1593	Special schools generally.	1697	Theory and practice of business.
1594	Law schools.	1698–1750	*blank.*

CLASS D.—HISTORY, GEOGRAPHY, TRAVEL.

Physical geography, 2711.
Biblical geography, 588.
Histories of subjects (as Religion, Literature, Medicine, etc.), see those subjects.

I. General Geography and Travels.

School geographies, 1556.
Biographies of travelers and discoverers, 2541–2.

1751 Geographical dictionaries; general gazetteers.
   For gazetteers of particular countries, see names of countries.
1752 Periodicals and transactions.
1753 Universal geography.
1754 Atlases and maps.
1755 Charts and hydrography.
1756 Ancient geography.
1757 Journeys round the world.
1758 Scientific voyages.
1759 Arctic exploration.
1760 Antarctic exploration.
1761 Collections of travels.
1762 Miscellaneous voyages and travels.
1763 General guide-books.
   For those of particular countries, see their names.
1764 Manuals of suggestions for travelers.
1765 Shipwrecks and disasters at sea.

II. Universal History.

1766 Philosophy of history.
1767 History of civilization.
1768 Universal histories.

III. Historical Collaterals.

Registration, 1416.
Censuses, see names of countries.

1769 Chronology.
1770 Statistics.
   For those of particular countries, see under their names.
1771 Ethnology. *Anthropology,* 2823.
1772 Prehistoric archæology.
1773 Antiquities generally.
1774   classical.
1775–1806 *blank.*
   Biblical antiquities, 587.
1807 Mythology generally.
1808   oriental.
1809   classical.
1810   Scandinavian.
1811   German.
1812–31 *blank.*
1832 Symbolism.
1833 Heraldry, precedence, titles of honor.
1834 Paleography, diplomatics.
1835 Numismatics.
1836 Manners and customs generally.
1837 Ceremonies generally.
   Religious rites, 925.
1838 Etiquette generally.
1839 Marriage customs.
1840 Sepulture.
   Cemeteries, 1408.
1841 Costume.
   Dress, toilet arts, 4255.
1842–72 Other customs.

IV. Ancient History.

History of Bible, 586.
Prehistoric archæology, 1772.
Antiquities, 1773, etc.

1873 Ancient history generally.
1874 Egypt.
1875 Eastern empires generally.
1876 Assyria, Babylon, Chaldea.
1877 Persia.
1878–96 *blank.*
1897 Jews.
   Judaism, 705.
   Medieval and modern Jews, 1958.
1898 Greece.
1899 Etruria.
1900 Rome generally.
   Roman law, 1827.
1901 Rome, regal and republican.
1902   empire.
1903   city.
1904 Byzantine empire.
1905–54 *blank.*

V. Medieval History.

1955 Middle Ages generally.
1956 Chivalry, feudal system
1957 Crusades.
1958 Medieval and modern Jews.
    Ancient Jews, 1897.
    Judaism, 705.
1959–78 *blank.*
    For medieval history of single countries, see their names.
    For medieval art, costume, philosophy, etc., see names of those subjects.

VI. Modern History and Europe.

1979 Modern history generally.
1980 Europe generally; geography.
1981   modern history.
1982   statistics.
1983   travels.
1984 England, general histories.
1985   *same*, compends.
1986   early period.
1987   Anglo-Saxon.
1988   conquest.
1989   conquest to Stuarts.
1990   Stuarts and Commonwealth.
1991   revolution to George I.
1992   Georges.
1993   recent history.
1994   local history.
1995   colonies.
1996   army and navy.
1997   public documents.
1998   statistics.
1999   travels.
2000   London
2001 Scotland; history.
2002   geography.
2003   travels.
2004 Ireland, history.
2005   geography.
2006   travels.
2007 Wales.
2008 France, history generally.
2009   *same*, compends.
2010   ancient.
2011   Louis XIV. to revolution.
2012   revolution.
2013   consulate and 1st empire.
2014   restoration.
2015   republic of 1848.
2016   second empire.
2017   war of 1870–1.
2018   third republic.
2019   geography and travels.
2020   Paris.
2021 Spain, history.
2022   Peninsular war.
2023   travels.
2024 Portugal.
2025 Italy, history.
2026   travels.
2027 Rome, modern.
2028 Switzerland.
2029   travels; Alps.
2030 Germany, history
2031   geography.
2032   travels.
2033 Prussia.
2034 German empire, new.
2035 Austria, history.
2036   geography and travels.
2037 Bohemia, history.
2038   geography and travels.
2039 Hungary, history.
2040   geography and travels.
2041 Holland, history.
2042   travels.
2043 Belgium.
2044 Scandinavia, history.
2045   travels.
2046 Norway.
2047 Sweden.
2048 Denmark.
2049 Iceland, Faroes.
2050 Poland, history.
2051   travels.
2052 Russia, history.
2053   geography and travels.
2054 Crimean war.
2055 Caucasus.
2056 Turkey, history.
2057   geography and travels.
2058 Greece, modern, history.
2059   geography and travels.
2060 Mediterranean and islands
2061–2100 *blank.*

VII Asia.

2101 East generally.
2102 Levant.

2103	Palestine.	2249	Algiers.
	geography, 588.	2250	Morocco.
2104	travels.	2251	Azores.
2105	Asia generally.	2252	Cape de Verde Islands. Canaries.
2106	Asia Minor.	2253	Madeira Islands.
2107	Syria.	2254	Cape Colony.
2108	Arabia.	2255	Madagascar.
2109	Persia, history.	2256–75	*blank.*
2110	geography and travels.	2276	Indian ocean and islands.
2111	Armenia.		
2112	Nestorians.		**IX. South Seas, Australasia, Islands.**
2113	Afghanistan and Beloochistan.		
2114	Mesopotamia.	2277	Australia.
2115	Turkestan.	2278	Van Diemen's Land.
2116	Hindostan, history.	2279	New Zealand.
2117	geography.	2280	Pacific Ocean and islands.
2118	travels.	2281	Sandwich Islands.
2119	Ceylon.	2282	Single islands and groups.
2120	East Indies generally.		
2121	Farther India generally.		**X. America, except the United States.**
2122	Burmah.		
2123	Siam.	2283	America generally, history.
2124	Cambodia.	2284	travels.
2125	Cochin China.	2285	North America, history.
2126	Sumatra.	2286	travels.
2127	Malacca.	2287	Indians.
2128	Java.	2288	Arctic America, Esquimaux.
2129	Borneo.	2289	Greenland.
2130	Archipelago.	2290	British America generally, history.
2131	China, history.	2291	travels.
2132	geography and travels.	2292	Canada, history.
2133	Thibet.	2293	travels.
2134	Japan and Formosa, history,	2294	Nova Scotia, history.
2135	geography and travels.	2295	travels.
2136	Tartary.	2296	New Brunswick, history.
2137	Siberia.	2297	travels.
2138–2237	*blank.*	2298	Newfoundland.
		2299	Other parts of British America.
	VIII. Africa.		*Russian America, see Alaska,* 2391.
		2300	West Indies generally.
2238	Africa generally.	2301	Cuba.
2239	western.	2302	Jamaica.
2240	eastern.	2303	St. Domingo and Hayti.
2241	southern.	2304	Mexico: history.
2242	inner.	2305	travels.
2243	Egypt, modern history.		*Mexican war; see under United States,*
	Antiquities and ancient history, 1874.		2333.
2244	travels.	2306	Central America.
2245	Nile explorations.	2307	South America generally.
2246	Abyssinia, history.	2308	Brazil.
2247	travels.	2309	Guiana.
2248	Barbary States generally.	2310	Venezuela, Ecuador.

2311 Peru.
2312 Bolivia.
2313 Chili.
2314 Argentine Republic.
2315 Buenos Ayres, United Provinces.
2316 Paraguay.
2317 Patagonia.
2318-27 *blank.*

XI. United States.

2328 History generally.
2329   compends.
2330 Settlement and colonial history.
2331 Stamp act, revolution.
2332 War of 1812.
2333 Mexican war.
2334 Slavery and abolition.
2335 Rebellion.
2336 Reconstruction.
2337 Political history.
2338 Military and naval history.
2339 Public documents.
2340 Statistics.
2341 Geography.
2342 Travels.
2343 Guide-books, gazetteers.
2344 Directories.
2345 New England, history.
2346   geography and travels.
2347 Southern states.
2348 Western states.
2349 Pacific coast.
2350 Maine.
2351 New Hampshire.
2352 Vermont.
2353 Massachusetts.
2354 Boston.
2355 Rhode Island.
2356 Connecticut.
2357 New York.
2358 New York City.
2359 New Jersey.
2360 Pennsylvania.
2361 Philadelphia.
2362 Delaware.
2363 Maryland.
2364 District of Columbia, Washington.
2365 Virginia.
2366 North Carolina.
2367 South Carolina.
2368 Georgia.
2369 Florida.
2370 Alabama.
2371 Mississippi.
2372 Louisiana.
2373 Texas.
2374 Arkansas.
2375 Tennessee.
2376 Kentucky.
2377 Ohio.
2378 Michigan.
2379 Indiana.
2380 Illinois.
2381 Missouri.
2382 Iowa.
2383 Wisconsin.
2384 Minnesota.
2385 Kansas and Nebraska.
2386 New Mexico, Arizona.
2387 Colorado, Nevada.
2388 Utah. *Mormonism,* 704.
2389 California.
2390 Oregon, Idaho, Washington Territory, etc.
2391 Alaska.
2392-2440 *blank.*

CLASS E.—BIOGRAPHY.

I. Collective Biography, General and National.

2441 General biographical dictionaries.
2442 Ancient biography.
2443 Modern biography.
2444 British biography.
2445 European biography.
2446 Single European nations.
2447 American.
2448-2500 *blank.*

II. Biography by Classes.

Actors, see Dramatists.
2501 Artists, collective.
2502   individual.
2503 Authors, collective.
2504   individual.

2505	Business men, collective	2531	Reformers, benefactors, collective.
2506	individual.	2532	individual.
2507	Christians (laics), collective.	2533	Royal and noble persons, collective.
2508	individual.	2534	individual.
2509	Clergy and missionaries, collective.	2535	Scientists, collective.
2510	individual.	2536	individual.
2511	Criminals, collective.	2537	Soldiers, naval men, sailors, collective.
2512	individual.	2538	individual.
	Criminal trials, 1365.	2539	Statesmen, collective.
2513	Dramatists and actors, collective.	2540	individual.
2514	individual.	2541	Travelers, discoverers, collective.
2515	Eccentrics, collective.	2542	individual.
2516	individual.	2543	Women, collective.
2517	Educators and teachers, collective.	2544	individual.
2518	individual.	2545–65	*blank.*
2519	Lawyers, judges, collective.		
2520	individual.		

III. Genealogy and Names.

Heraldry, 1833.

2566	Genealogical periodicals and collections.
2567	individual names.
2568	Epitaphs, baptismal registers, other records
2569	Names of persons.
2570	Names of places.
2571–90	*blank.*

2521	Mechanics and inventors, collective.
2522	individual.
2523	Musicians and composers, collective.
2524	individual.
2525	Philosophers, collective.
2526	individual.
2527	Physicians, collective.
2528	individual.
2529	Poets, collective.
2530	individual.

CLASS F.—SCIENCE.

Natural theology, 855.
Religion and science, 865.
Geology and religion, 865.
Scientific schools, 1510, 1597.
Special education, 1508, 1593.
Biographies of scientific men, 2535–6.

I. General Treatises.

2591	Encyclopedias and dictionaries.
2592	Transactions and journals.
2593	Histories, general.

II. Mathematics.

School books, 1554–5.

2594	Histories.
2595	Transactions and journals.
2596	General treatises.
2597	Arithmetic.
2598	Algebra.
2599	Geometry.
2600	Trigonometry.
2601	Calculus.
2602	Quaternions.
2603	Probabilities.
2604	Logarithms, tables.
2605–24	*blank.*

III. Natural Philosophy.

School books, 1561
School apparatus, 1564.
Philosophical-instrument making, 3913.

2625	Dictionaries, encyclopedias.

2626 Periodicals and transactions.
2627 Histories.
2628 General treatises.
2629 Mechanics.
2630 Hydrostatics.
2631 Pneumatics.
2632 Acoustics.
2633 Optics.
2634 Spectroscopy.
2635 Heat.
2636 Electricity.
2637 Electric light.
2638 Magnetism, galvanism.
2639 Molecular mechanics.
2640–90 *blank.*

IV. Astronomical Science.

Almanacs, 5901.
2691 Astronomy, history.
2692   journals, transactions.
2693   general treatises.
2694–2710 *blank.*
2711 Navigation.
2712 Geodesy.
2713 Astrology.
2714 *blank.*

V. Cosmology.

2715 Cosmology generally.
    Metaphysically, 1222.
2716 Physical geography.
    Scientific voyages, 1758.
    Arctic explorations, 1759.
    Antarctic explorations, 1760.
2717 Volcanoes.
2718 Tides.
2719 Meteorology.
2720 Aeronautics.
2721–30 *blank.*

VI. Geology.

Geology and religion, 865.
Agricultural geology, 4028.
Mining, 3810–11.
2731 Encyclopedias, dictionaries.
2732 Periodicals and transactions.
2733 General treatises.
2734 Paleontology.
2735 Dynamical geology.
2736 Local treatises by countries, etc.

2737–2746 *blank.*
2747 Mineralogy.
2748–57 *blank.*
2758 Crystallography.
2759 Precious stones.
2760–89 *blank.*

VII. Chemistry.

Toxicology, 3522.
Applied chemistry, 3867.
Agricultural chemistry, 4028.
2790 Dictionaries.
2791 Periodicals and transactions.
2792 Histories.
2793 General treatises.
2794 Inorganic chemistry.
2795 Organic chemistry.
2796 Chemical analysis generally.
2797   qualitative.
2798   quantitative.
2799 Alchemy.
2800–2819 *blank.*

VIII. General Natural History; Zoology.

Biblical natural history, 589.
Domestic animals, 4141–8.
Paleontology, 2734.
2820 General natural histories; encyclopedias.
2821 General zoology.
2822 Periodicals and transactions.
2823 Anthropology.
    Biology, metaphysically, 1223.
    Ethnology, 1771.
2824 Evolution, Darwinism.
2825 Instinct and reason of animals.
2826 Local fauna.
2827–2926 *blank.*
2927 Comparative anatomy.
    Human anatomy, 3216.
    Art anatomy, 4400.
2928 Vertebrates.
2929 Mammals.
2930 Birds.
2931 Reptiles.
2932 Fishes.
2933 Invertebrates generally.
    Agricultural pests, 4031.
2934 Articulates.
2935 Mollusks.
2936 Radiates, protozoa.

2937 Microscopy.
2938 Taxidermy.
2939 Collectors' manuals.
2940–3000 *blank.*

IX. Botany.

Gardening, 4032.
Cultivated plants, 4033–4139.
Paleontology, 2734.

3001 Encyclopedias.
3002 Periodicals and transactions.
3003 History.
3004 General treatises.
3005 Local floras.
3006–3104 *blank.*
3105 Special plants.
3106–3204 *blank.*
3205 Medical botany.
3206–10 *blank.*

X. General Medicine.

Medical botany, 3205.
Medical schools, 1595.
Medical biography, 2527–8.

3211 Encyclopedias and dictionaries.
3212 Periodicals and transactions.
3213 Histories.
3214 General treatises.
3215 Compends.
3216 Human anatomy.
  Comparative anatomy, 2927.
  Art anatomy, 4400.
3217 Human physiology.
  Mind and body, 1277.
  Sleep and dreams, 1282.
  Physiognomy, 1281.
  Animal magnetism, 1283.
3218–37 *blank.*

XI. Hygiene.

Public health, 1405.
Prostitution, administratively, 1406.
Sewerage, 3662.

3238 Periodicals and transactions.
3239 General treatises.
3240 Dietetics.
3241 Exercise.
  Athletic sports, 4533–41.
  Gymnastics and calisthenics, 4534.

3242 Stimulants and narcotics generally.
  Morals of use of, 1290.
3243 Alcoholic liquors.
3244 Tobacco.
3245 Opium.
3246–65 *blank.*

XII. Medical Practice.

Veterinary medicine, 4142.

3266 Encyclopedias and dictionaries.
3267 Periodicals and transactions.
3268 General treatises.
3269 Compends.
3270 Materia medica, pharmaceutics.
  Medical botany, 3205.
3271 Hospitals, dispensaries.
3272 Nursing.
3273 Yellow-fever.
3274 Cholera.
3275 Diseases of ear and eye.
  Blind asylums, 1604.
  Deaf and dumb asylums, 1603.
3276 Diseases of throat and lungs.
3277 Children's diseases.
3278 Women's diseases.
3279 Insanity; lunatic asylums.
3280–3379 Other special diseases.
3380 Water cure.
3381 Health resorts.
3382 Homeopathy.
3383–3403 Other medical systems.
3404 Sanitary commissions.
3405 Quacks and quackery.
3406–15 *blank.*

XIII. Surgical Practice.

3416 Surgery generally.
3417 Military surgery.
3418 Obstetrics.
3419 Dentistry.
3420 Anæsthetics.
3421–3520 *blank.*

XIV. Medical Jurisprudence.

3521 General treatises.
3522 Toxicology.
3523 Medical ethics.
3524–33 *blank.*

CLASS G.—ARTS AND TRADES.

Schools of technology, 1598.
Biographies of inventors and mechanics, 2551-2.

I. General Treatises.

3534 Encyclopedias and dictionaries.
3535 Periodicals and transactions.
3536 Histories.
3537 General technologies.
3538 Exhibitions.

II. Engineering.

Military engineering, 3730.

3539 Encyclopedias and dictionaries.
3540 Periodicals and transactions.
3541 General treatises.
3542 Mechanical engineering.
3543 Topographical engineering.
3544 Steam engineering.
    Steamships, steam navigation, 3756.
3545 Railroad engineering.
3546 Canal and harbor engineering.
3547 Hydraulic engineering.
3548 Diving bells, diving armor.
3549 Mensuration, surveying, leveling.
    Geodesy, 2712.
3550 Instruments, field-books.
3551 Manuals, tables.
3552-71 *blank.*

III. Architecture, Building.

Lighting, 3915-17.
Warming and ventilation, 3914.
Bricks and tiles, 3875.
Mortars and cements, 3876.
Decorative art, 4401.
Furniture, 3909.
School architecture, 1562.

3572 Encyclopedias an dictionaries.
3573 Periodicals and transactions.
3574 Histories.
3575 Ancient architecture.
3576 Oriental architecture.
3577 Egyptian architecture.
3578 Greek architecture.
3579 Roman architecture.
3580 Modern architecture.
3581 Church architecture and ecclesiology.
3582 Domestic architecture.
3583-3606 *blank.*
3607 Building generally.
3608 Masonry.
3609 Carpentry.
3610 Stairs and rails.
3611 Bridge-building.
3612-61 *blank.*
3662 House plumbing, sewerage.
3663 Iron buildings.
3664-3712 *blank.*

IV. Military Arts.

Military law, courts-martial, 1358.
Military schools, 1599.
Military biography, 2537-8.

3713 Dictionaries.
3714 Periodicals and transactions.
3715 Military history.
3716 Art of war.
3717 Strategy and tactics.
3718 Fire-arms, ordnance.
    Sporting guns, 4558.
    Gun-making, 3907.
3719-29 *blank.*
3730 Military engineering.
3731 Fortification.
3732-51 *blank.*

V. Naval Arts.

Naval schools, 1599.
Yachting, boating, 4536.
Biographies of sailors and naval men, 2537-8.
Navigation, 2711.

3752 History of ships and navigation.
3753 Ship-building.
3754 Iron ships, iron-clad vessels.
3755 Seamanship.
3756 Steamships, steam navigation.
3757 Naval war.
3758 Wrecking, life-saving.
3759 Lighthouses, light-ships.
3760-3800 *blank.*

VI. Mechanic Arts and Trades.

Lace-making, 4257.
Needlework, 4256.
Ornamental work, 4258, *etc.*
Manual-labor schools, 1601.
Technological schools, 1598.
Mechanics (science), 2629.

3801 Encyclopedias and dictionaries.
3802 Periodicals, transactions.
3803 Annual reports.
3804 Public documents.
3805 General treatises; technologies.
3806 Exhibitions.
3807 Industrial history.
3808 Machinery.
3809 Inventions, patents.
  Patent law, 1367.
3810 Mines, mining, quarrying.
  Mining corporations, 1635.
3811 Coal, coal-mining.
3812 Petroleum.
3813 Metal-working generally.
3814 Metallurgy.
3815 Assaying.
3816–66 Metals separately.
3867 Applied chemistry generally.
3868 Dyeing.
3869 Tanning.
3870 Perfumery.
3871 Soaps.
3872 Distilling, brewing.
3873 Glass-making.
  Glass-painting, 4407.
3874 Pottery and porcelain.
3875 Bricks, tiles, terra cotta.
3876 Mortars and cements.
3877 Manufacturing generally.
3878 Textile fabrics generally.
3879 Woolen manufacture.
3880 Cotton manufacture.
3881–3900 Other textile fabrics.
3901 Rubber and gutta-percha goods.
3902 Saddlery, harness-making.
3903 Shoe and boot trade.
3904 Clothes-making.
3905 Blacksmithing.
3906 Lock-making.
3907 Gun-making.
3908 Carriage-making.
3909 Cabinet-making, furniture.
  School furniture, 1568.
3910 Upholstering.
3911 Turning.
3912 Clock and watch making.
3913 Philosophical instrument making.
3914 Warming and ventilation.
3915 Illumination generally.
3916 Gas-making, gas-fitting.
3917 Printing.
3918 Bookbinding.
3919 Telegraphy.
3920 Telephone.
3921 Photography, sun-pictures generally.
3922–4022 *blank.*

VII. Agriculture.

4023 Encyclopedias and dictionaries.
4024 Periodicals and transactions.
4025 Public documents.
4026 Histories.
4027 General treatises.
4028 Agricultural chemistry and geology.
4029 Drainage.
4030 Manures.
4031 Pests and hindrances.
4032 Flower-gardening.
4033 Kitchen and market gardening.
4034 Fruit culture generally.
4035 Grapes, wines.
4036 Cane, sugars.
4037 Mulberry, silkworm.
4038 Cotton culture.
4039 Tree culture, forestry.
4040–4139 Other special plants.
4140 Landscape-gardening.
  Parks, public gardens (administration), 1407.
4141 Domestic animals generally.
4142 Veterinary medicine.
4143 Horse, horse-shoeing.
4144 Horned cattle.
4145 Dairying.
4146 Sheep.
4147 Poultry.
4148 Bees; honey.
4149 Fish culture.
4150 Fisheries.
4151 Dogs.
4152 Cage birds.
4153–4252 *blank.*

VIII. Domestic Arts.

Hygiene, 3238, *etc.*
Domestic architecture, 3582.
Children's diseases, 3277.
Nursing, 3272.

4253 Domestic economy generally.
4254 Cookery and food.
    Dietetics, 3240.
4255 Dress, toilet arts.
    Costume historically, 1841.
4256 Needle-work; embroidery.
4257 Lace-making.
4258 Wax flowers.
4259 Scroll-sawing; Sorrento-work.
4260–80. Other ornamental work.

IX. Fine Arts.

Æsthetics, 5554.
Criticism, 5555–60.
Symbolism, 1832.
Architecture, 3572, *etc.*
Art education, 1512
Photography, 3921.
Biography of artists, 2501–2.

4281 Encyclopedias and dictionaries.
4282 Periodicals and transactions.
4283 General treatises.
4284 Compends.
4285 General histories.
4286 Ancient art generally.
4287 Oriental art (ancient).
4288 Egyptian art.
4289 Greek art.
4290 Roman art.
4291 Christian art.
4292 Renaissance art.
4293 Modern art generally.
4294 Oriental art (modern).
4295 Chinese art.
4296 Japanese art.
4297–4347 *blank.*
4348 Sculpture, carving.
4349 Painting; history.
4350   Materials and methods.
4351   Italian schools.
4352–61 *blank.*
4362   Flemish schools.
4363   Dutch schools.
4364–73 German schools.
4374–83 French schools.
4384–93 English schools.
4394   American schools.
4395   Water-colors.
4396 Drawing and designing generally.
4397 Free-hand drawing.
4398 Perspective drawing.
4399 Mechanical drawing.
4400 Art anatomy.
4401 Decorative art and ornamental design generally.
    Ornamental work, 4256, *etc.*
4402   ancient ornament
4403   medieval ornament.
4404   modern ornament.
4405 Lettering.
4406 Illumination.
4407 Glass-painting.
4408 Engraving generally.
4409 Wood-engraving
4410 Copper and steel engraving.
4411 Etching.
4412 Books of prints, galleries.
4413–63 *blank.*

X. Music.

Biography of musicians and composers, 2523–4

4464 Encyclopedias and dictionaries.
4465 Periodicals and transactions.
4466 History.
4467 Composition; musical education.
4468 Collections; general, and secular music.
4469   sacred music.
4470 Operas.
4471 Oratorios.
4472 Single instrumental compositions.
4473 Songs with music
4474 Treatises on singing; vocal training.
4475 Pianoforte, history.
4476   instruction books.
4477 Violin, history.
4478   instruction books.
4479 Organ, history.
4480   instruction books.
4481–4530 Other single instruments.

XI. Recreations.

Morals of amusements, 1289.
Private theatricals, 5607.

4531 Periodicals.
4532 General treatises.
4533 Athletic sports generally.
    Exercise, 3241.
4534 Gymnastics, calisthenics.
4535 Fencing, boxing, wrestling.
4536 Yachting, rowing.
4537 Horsemanship, driving, racing.
4538 Swimming.
4539 Dancing.
4540 Ball-play.
4541 Croquet, lawn tennis.
4542 Field sports generally.
4543 Hunting; sporting guns and tackle.
    Gun-making, 3907.
4544 Trapping.
4545 Angling; fishing tackle.
4546 Table and parlor games generally.
4547 Chess.
4548 Billiards.
4549 Whist.
4550–70 Other games at cards.
4571–90 Other games.
4591 Sleight of hand, conjuring.
4592 Ventriloquism.
4593–4620 *blank.*

CLASS H.—LITERATURE.

Copyright, copyright law, 1868.

I. History of Literature.

Bible and biblical literature, Class A, Chap. I.
Biography of authors, 2503–4.
Paleography, diplomatics, 1834.

4621 History of literature generally.
4622 History of the drama generally.
4623 History of poetry generally.
4624 History of fiction generally.
4625 History of periodical literature.
4626 History of ancient literature generally.
4627 History of Greek literature generally.
4628 History of Roman literature generally.
4629–48 Other ancient literature.
4649 History of oriental literature.
4650 History of medieval literature.
4651 History of modern literature.
4652 History of English literature.
4653 History of American literature.
4654 History of French literature.
4655 History of German literature.
4656 History of Italian literature.
4657 History of Spanish literature.
4658 History of Portuguese literature.
4659–4708 *blank.*

II. Philology.

Names of persons, 2569.
Names of places, 2570.

4709 Periodicals and transactions.
4710 Comparative philology.
4711 Asiatic languages generally.
4712 Semitic languages generally.
4713–17 Hebrew.
4718–22 Chaldee.
4723–27 Arabic.
4728–32 Cuneiform languages.
4733–37 Syriac.
4738–42 Zend.
4743–47 Persian.
4748 Indo-Germanic languages generally.
4749–53 Sanscrit.
4754–8 Pali and other derivatives of Sanscrit.
4759–63 Dravidian languages.
4764 Other Hindostan languages.
4765–9 Chinese.
4770–4 Japanese.
4775–4800 Other Asiatic languages.
4801–30 Pacific island languages.
4831–5 Egyptian, Coptic.
4836–40 Ethiopic.
4841–83 Other African languages.
4884–93 Greek language.
4894–4903 Latin language.
4904–4913 German language.
4914–28 Dutch language.
4924–33 Scandinavian languages.
4934 Celtic languages generally.
4935–44 Gaelic language.
4945–54 Irish (Erse) language.
4955–64 Welsh.
4965–84 Slavonic languages.
4985 Ugro-Altaic languages.
4986–95 Turkish language.

4996–5005	Hungarian language.
5006–15	Finnish language.
5016–25	Anglo-Saxon language.
5026	English : History.
5027	Grammar
5028	Orthography.
5029	Etymology.
5030	Dictionaries.
5031	Synonyms and antonyms.
5032	Prosody and versification.
5033	Dialects.
5034	French : history.
5035	Courses and methods.
5036	Grammar.
5037	Orthography.
5038	Etymology.
5039	Dictionaries.
5040	Synonyms and antonyms.
5041	Prosody and versification.
5042	Dialects.
5043	Provençal language.
5044–53	Spanish.
5054–63	Portuguese.
5064–73	Italian.
5074–5124	North American languages.
5125–5144	Mexican and Central American languages.
5145–5230	South American languages.
5231–5530	*blank.*

III. Linguistics.

School-books, 1558–61.

5531	Universal language.
5532	General grammar.
5533	Alphabets.
5534	Composition.
5535	Punctuation.
5536	Elocution; reading.
	Reading-books, 1558.
	Preaching, 1932.
5537	Rhetoric.
	Oratory, 5721–35.
5538	Prosody and versification.
	and see under separate languages.
5539	Mnemonics.
5540	Penmanship.
5541	Phonography.
5542	Other short-hand systems.
5543	Phonetic reform.
5544–53	*blank.*

IV. Critical Science.

5554	Æsthetics generally.
5555	Criticism generally.
5556	Criticism of literature.
5557	Criticism of poetry.
5558	Criticism of drama.
5559	Criticism of painting and sculpture.
5560	Criticism of music.

V. Poetry.

History of poetry, 4623.
Criticism of poetry, 5557.
Hymnology, 964.
Prosody and versification, 5528.
Biographies of poets, 2529–30.

5561	English poetry, general collections.
5562	songs and ballads, collections.
5563	sonnets, collections.
	Songs with music, 4478.
5564	Scottish poetry, collections.
5565	Irish poetry, collections.
5566	American poetry, collections.
5567	American songs and ballads, collections.
5568	Humorous poetry in English.
5569	Works in English, of single poetical writers.
5570	Epigrams and acrostics in English.
5571	Greek poetry.
5572	Latin poetry.
5573	Macaronic poetry.
5574	Anglo-Saxon poetry.
5575	Gaelic, Welsh, Erse poetry.
5576	German poetry.
5577	Dutch poetry.
5578	Slavonic poetry.
5579	Scandinavian poetry.
5580	French poetry.
5581	Italian poetry.
5582	Spanish poetry.
5583	Portuguese poetry.
5584	Arabic poetry.
5585	Persian poetry.
5586–90	Other oriental poetry.
5591–5600	Other poetry.

VI. Drama.

Dramatic criticism, 5558.
History of drama, 4622.
Dramatic biographies, 2513–14.

5601	Dramatic theory; acting.

5602 English dramatists; collections and complete works.
5603 Single English dramas.
5604 Shakespeare; editions.
5605   comments.
5606 Shakespeariana.
5607 Private threatricals.
5608 Dramatic works in French.
5609   German.
5610   Spanish.
5611   Portuguese.
5612   Italian.
5613   Greek.
5614   Latin.
5615–64 Dramatic works in other languages.

VII. Fiction.

History of fiction, 4624.
Criticism of fiction, 5556.
Mythology, 1807–12.
Religious fiction and allegory, 968.

5665 Collections of novels in English.
5666 Novels and tales in English.
5667   French.
5668   German.
5669   Italian.
5670   Spanish.
5671–95 Other languages.
5696 Fables.
5697 Legends and fairy stories.
5698 Stories for young persons.
5699–5720 *blank.*

VIII. Oratory.

Rhetoric, 5537.
Elocution, 5536.
Vocal training, 4474.

5721 General works on oratory.
5722 Speeches and addresses, collections.
5723 Complete works of orators.
5724 Single speeches and addresses, political.
    obituary, see Biography.
5725 Fourth of July orations.
5726–35 *blank.*

IX. Collections; Books for Entertainment.

For collections, whole works, essays, letters, etc., on particular subjects, see under names of such subjects.

5736 Whole works of authors.
5737 Correspondence.
5738 Essays.
5739 Lectures.
5740 Sketches and short articles, collections.
5741 Selections and beauties.
5742 Quotations.
5743 Dialogues and conversations.
5744 Proverbs.
5745 Maxims.
5746 Emblems.
5747 Anecdotes.
    Religious anecdotes, 969.
5748 Ana.
5749 Table-talk.
5750 Jests, puns, facetious sayings.
5751 Puzzles, (conundrums, riddles, charades, anagrams, rebuses, etc.)
5752 Comic prose writings.
    Humorous poetry, 5568.
5753 Satires and parodies in prose.
    Same in verse, 5568.
5754 Entertaining collections.
5755–5800. Other collections.

X. Periodicals.

Periodicals and transactions on special subjects are under the names of such.
History of periodicals, 4625.

5801 Magazines.
5802–50 *blank.*
5851 Newspapers.
5852–5900 *blank.*
5901 Almanacs.
5901–50 Other annuals.

XI. Encyclopedic Works.

For those on special subjects, see such subjects.

5951 Encyclopedias.
5952–6000 Other collections of useful knowledge.

XII. Bibliography.

6001 Bibliographical periodicals.
6002 General bibliographies.

6003 Bibliographies by single countries.
6004–54 *blank.*
6055 Bibliographies on separate subjects.
6056–6155 *blank.*
6156 Book rarities.
6157–66 *blank.*
6167 Publishers' lists.
6168–6216 *blank.*
6217 Trade sales.
6218 Catalogues of second-hand book dealers.
6219–6268 *blank.*

6269 Book auction sale catalogues.
6270–6320 *blank.*

XIII. Libraries.

6321 Library history and management.
6322–41 *blank.*
6342 Library reports.
6343–62 *blank.*
6363 Library catalogues.
6364–83 *blank.*
6384 Cataloguing.

ALPHABET OF TOPICS.

NOTE.—A certain number of topics not provided for specially in the classification are left to be numbered at the places left blank, as may be convenient.

Abolition	1465	geology	4028	history	2285
Aborigines, North American,		implements	4153	languages	5074–124
history	2287	Agriculture	4023–4252	travels	2286
languages	5074–124	encyclopedias	4023	America, South	2307
Abortion	3418	periodicals and transactions		geography	2307
Absolutism	1395	tions	4024	history	2307
Abyssinia, history	2246	reports	4025	languages	5145–230
language	4836–40	pests and hindrances.	4031	travels	2307
travels	2247	Air	2719	American antiquities	2383
Academies, educational	1591	Alabama	2370	biography	2447
of science	2592	Alaska	2391	fine arts	4394
Academy (Platonist)	1039	Albania	2057	languages	5074–5530
Accounts	1695	Albertypes	3921	literature	4653
Acoustics	2632	Albigenses	625	philosophy	1118
Acrostics	5570	Alchemy	2799	poetry	5566–7
Acting	5601	Alcoholic liquors	3243	revolution	2331
Actors, lives of	2513–14	morals of using	1290	slavery	1465
Acts, legislative, see names		Ales	3872	songs and ballads	5567
of countries, states, etc.		Alexandrian philosophy	1045	Americanisms	5033
Acts of the Apostles	506, 515	Algæ	3105	Amputation	3416–17
Addresses, collections of	5722–3	Algebra	2598	Amusements	4531–4620
single	5724–5	Algeria	2249	morals of	1289
Administration	1395–1433	Aliens	1329	Ana	5748
Admiralty law	1856	Allegories	5696	Anagrams	5751
Adult education	1518	religious	968	Anæsthetics	3420
Adultery	1413	Alloys	3814	Analysis, chemical	2796
Advent, second	883	Almanacs	5901	qualitative	2797
Advertising	1697	statistical	1770	quantitative	2798
Aerolites	2693	Alphabets	5533	Analytical geometry	2599
Aeronautics	2720	ornamental	4405	Anatomy, art	4400
Æsthetics	5554	Amateur theatricals	5607	comparative	2927
Æthiopia, see Abyssinia		Ambassadors	1325	human	3216
Æthiopic language	4836–40	Ambrotypes	3921	Ancient architecture	3575
Affections	1224	America; history	2283	art	4286–91
Afghanistan	2113	travels	2284	geography	1756
Africa	2238–76	America, Central	2306	history	1873–1978
African colonization	1462	languages	5125–44	Jews	1897
languages	4841–83	America, North	2285–2440	law	1326
Agricultural chemistry	4028	geography	2286	literature	4626–48

ornament	4402	poetry	5584	Artillery	3718
philosophy	1004–1071	Arboriculture	4039	Artists, lives of	2501–2
Anecdotes	5747	Archæology generally	1773	Arts and trades	3801–4022
business	1697	prehistoric	1772	dictionaries	3801
religious	969	Archery	4953	encyclopedias	3801
Aneurism	3416	Archipelago, East Indian	2130	exhibitions	3608
Angels	886	Greek	2059	history of	3807
Anglican church	630	Architects, lives	2501–2	periodicals and transac-	
Angling	4545	Architectural drawing	4396	tions	3802
Anglo-Saxon history	1987	Architecture	3572–3712	reports	3803–4
language	5016–25	ancient	3575	Arts, fine. *See* Art.	
literature	4652	church	3581	Ashantee	2239
poetry	5574	dictionaries	3572	Asia	2101–2237
Animal magnetism	1283	domestic	3582	ecclesiastical history	616
Animals	2820–2936	history	3574	history	2105
domestic	4141–49	modern	3580	travels	2105
Bible	589	naval	3753	Asia Minor	2106
Animalculæ	2936	oriental	3576	travels	2106
Annuals (publications)	5754	periodicals and transac-		Asiatic languages	4711
Annuities	1693	tions	3573	Assassination	1357
Anonyms	6055	school	1562	Assassins	1440
Antarctic explorations	1760	Arctic regions	2288	Assault and battery	1357
Anthropology	2823	explorations	1759	Assaying	3815
Antilles	2300–3	Argentine republic	2314	Assent	1203
Anti-Masonry	1441	Arianism	853	Associations	1436–7, 1440–58
Antinomianism	853	Aristocracy	1395	business	1634–86
Antiquities	1773	Aristotelian philosophy	1040	charitable	1409
biblical	587	Arithmetic	2597	musical	4465–6
classical	1774	Arizona	2386	religious	933–60
Antiquity of man	1771–2	Arkansas	2374	Assurance	1692–4
Aphorisms	5744–5	Armenia	2111	Assyria	1876
Apocalypse	515, 882	Armenian church	616	Assyrian language	4728–32
Apocrypha	509–11	language	4775	Asthma	3276
Apologetics	866	Armies	3713–17	Astrology	2713
Apophthegms	5744–5	Arminianism	639	Astronomical maps	2693
Apoplexy	3280	Armor	3715	Astronomical observations	2693
Apostles	614	Army, British	1996	Astronomy	2691–2710
Apostolic church	614	U. S.	2338	descriptive	2693
succession	619, 630	Art	4281–4463	Asylums, blind	1604
Apparatus (school philosoph-		anatomy	4400	deaf and dumb	1603
ical)	1564	ancient	4286	lunatic	3279
Apparitions	1284	Christian	4291	orphan	940
Apples	4040	criticism of	5555–60	Atheism	858–9
Applied chemistry	3867	decorative	4401	Athens	1898, 2058
Applied mathematics	2596	education	1512	Athletic sports	4533–41
Aquariums	4153	encyclopedias	4281	Atlases	1754
Aquatint	4413	history	4285	Atmosphere	2719
Aqueducts	3547	periodicals	4282	Atonement	877
Arabia	2108	Artesian wells	3922	Aurora	2719
Arabian language	4723–7	Articulates, paleontology	2734	Australasia	2277–9
philosophy	1101	zoology	2934	Australia	2277

Austria, history	2035	concordances	590	(natural science)	2820
travels	2036	criticism	513–84	Birds, cage	4152
Authors, dramatic, lives of	2513–4	dictionaries and encyclopedias	585	paleontology	2734
poetical, lives of	2529–30	English	3	zoology	2930
prose, lives of	2503–4	exegesis	513–84	Birth	3418
Autobiography, see Biography.		geography	588	Blacksmithing	3905
Autocracy	1395	history of	586	Bleaching	3878
Ava	2122	in schools	1520	Blind, asylums	1604
Azores	2251	inspiration of	867–8	education of	1604
Aztecs	2304	natural history	589	printing for	1604
		societies	937	Blindness	3275
Babylon	1876	texts	1–508	Block books	6055
Backgammon	4571	translations and versions	4–504	Blowpipe	2796
Baconian philosophy	2628	Bibliography	6001–6320	Blue laws	1331, 2356
Ball play	4540	Billiards	4548	Boating	4536
Ballads	5562, 5567	Biography	2441–2565	Boats	3753, 4536
Ballooning	2720	actors	2513–14	Body and mind	1277–84
Bank note engraving	4410	American	2447	Bohemia	2037–8
Bankrupt laws	1355	ancient	2442	Bokhara	2115
Banks, banking	1687	artists	2501–2	Bolivia	2312
Baptism	929–30	authors	2503–4	Bonds and stocks	1689
Baptismal registers	2568	British	2444	Bones	2927, 3216
Baptists	640	business men	2505–6	Books (literature)	4621–6384
Bar, legal	1323	Christians (lay)	2507–8	Book binding	3918
Barbary States	2248	clergy	2509–10	collecting	6156
Barometer	2719	criminals	2511–12	keeping	1695
Bas-reliefs	4348	dictionaries	2441	rarities	6156
Base ball	4540	dramatists	2513–14	Books of prints	4212
Basque language	5231	eccentrics	2515–16	Booksellers' catalogues	6167–6320
provinces	2021, 2023	European	2445–6	Boot-making	3908
Baths	3246	lawyers and judges	2519–20	Borneo	2129
Bavaria	2030, 2032	mechanics and inventors	2521–2	Boston	2354
Beauties (selections)	5741			Botany, fossil	2734
Beauty, the beautiful	5554	modern	2448	local floras	3005
Beer	3872	musicians	2523–4	medical	3205
Bees	4148	philosophers	2525–6	periodicals and transactions	3002
Beetles	2934	physicians	2527–8		
Beets	4040	poets	2529–30	special plants	3105
sugar	4036	reformers and benefactors	2531–2	systematic	3004
Belgium	2043			Boxing	4535
Belles-lettres	5554–5950	royal and noble	2533–4	Brahmanism	707
Bell-ringing	4481	scientists	2535–6	Brandy	3872
Bells	3922	soldiers and naval men	2537–8	Brazil, history	2308
Beloochistan	2113			travels	2308
Bermudas	2300	statesmen	2539–40	Breviaries	962
Bible	1–610	travelers and discoverers	2541–2	Brewing	3872
Bible, aids to study	511–610			Bricks	3875
antiquities	587	women	2543–4	Bridge-building	3611
biography	591	Biology (metaphysics)	1223	Brigands	413
commentaries	513–88			British America	2290–1

army	1996	Canon of Scriptures	512	Chances	2603
biography	2444	Capital and labor	1470	Character	1287
Columbia	2299	Capital punishment	1414–15	Charades	5751
India	2116–19	Car-building	3609	Charitable associations	1409
Museum	6321	Cards, games at	4549–70	Charities, public	1409
navy	1996	Caribbee Islands	2300	religious	940
Britons	1986	Caricatures	4293	Charts, geographical	1755
Bronchitis	3276	Carpentry	3609	historical	1769
Bronzes	4348	Carpets	3881	Chasing	4348
Buccaneers	2300, 1762	Carriage making	3908	Checkers	4571
Buddhism	710	Cartesianism	1103	Cheese	4145
Buenos Ayres	2315	Carthage	1905	Chemical analysis	2796–8
Building	3607–3712	Carving and chasing	4348	technology	3867
Building associations	1474	Cashmere	2116	Chemicals, manufacture of	3867
Bulgaria	2056	Castile	2021	Chemistry, agricultural	4028
Burial	1840	Casting, founding	3813	analytical	2796–8
Burial clubs	1476	Casts	4348	applied	3867
Burmah	2122	Casuistry	619	inorganic	2794
Business	1628–1750	Catacombs	1840	manufacturing	3867
colleges	1600	Catalogues of books	6167–6320	organic	2795
ethics	1291	book sales	6217–20	Chess	4547
manuals	1696	libraries	6363–83	Childbirth	3418
theory and practice	1697	Cataloguing	6384	Children, diseases of	3277
Butter	4145	Catarrh	3280	education of, see Education.	
Butterflies	2934	Catechisms	854	Chili	2313
Byzantine empire	1904	Cathedrals	3581	Chimneys	3582
Byzantium	1904	Catholic Church	618–23	China, history	2131
		Cattle	4144	travels	2132
Cabinet making	3909	Caucasus	2055	Chinese language	4765–9
Cage birds	4152	Caucus	1396	literature	4659
Calabria	2025	Cavalry	3716	religion	711–15
Calculators	2597	Cave-men; cave-hunting	1772	Chivalry	1956
Calculus (mathematics)	2601	Caves	2733	Chloroform	3420
Caledonia	2001	Celibacy	617	Cholera	3274
California	2389	Celtic language	4934–64	Christ, doctrine of	875–7
Calisthenics	4534	literature	4650	life of	875
Caloric	2635	poetry	5575	Christian art	4291
Calvinism	629	Celts	1771	associations	941
Cambists	1696	Cements	3876	church	611–700
Cambria	2007	Cemeteries	1408, 1840	doctrines	851–920
Cameos	4348	Censuses, see names of countries.		ethics	967
Campbellism	637			fathers	615
Camping out	1764	Central Africa	2242	institutions	921–60
Canada	2292–3	America	2306	life	966
Canal engineering	3546	Ceramic art	3874	polity	921–60
of Suez	3546	Ceremonies	1837–72	unions	941
transit	1633	religious	925	Christianity,	612–701, 851–1000
Canary Isles	2252	Cetacea	2929	evidences	866
Cancer	3280	Ceylon	2119	history	612–701
Cane sugar	4036	Chaldea	1876	Christians, biography of	2507–10
Canon law	1238	Chaldee language	4718–22	Christmas; customs	925

Christology	875–7	Coleoptera	2934	Complete works	5736
Chromolithography	4413	Collected travels	1761	Composition, literary	5534
Chronology	1769	works	5736	musical	4467
Church	612–700, 921–60	" (religious)	993	Comte's philosophy	1115
and schools	1520	Collections, art	4283	Conchology	2935
and State	924	drawing and design	4401	Concordances to authors, see	
apostolic	614	engraving	4408	their names.	
architecture	3581	entertaining	5754	Concordances to Bible	590
of England	630	of music	4468–9	Confectionery	4254
fathers	615	of poetry	5561–8	Confessional	619
history	612–700	of sermons	994	Confucianism	711
music	4469	of useful knowledge	5952	Congregationalism	638
polity	921–60	painting	4412	Conic sections	2599
of Rome	618–23	photography	3921	Conjuring	4591
Churchyards	1840, 1408	sculpture	4348	Connecticut	2356
Circassia	2055	technological	3538	Conscience	1225, 1286
Circumnavigations	1757	Collectors' manuals (natu-		Conservatories (gardening)	4032
Citizenship	1395	ral history)	2939	" of music	4467
City transit	1633	College songs	4478	Constantinople	2056
Civil engineering	3539–71	Colleges and universities	1592	Constitution, English	1330
law	1327	" business	1600	United States	1331
service reform	1433	Collieries	3811	Constitutional law	1329–31
" regulations	1400	Colombia, S. A.	2318	Construction, architectural	
trials	1866	Colonial history of U. S.	2330		3580, 3607
Civilization	1767	Colonial system	1461	Consuls, foreign	1325
Clairvoyance	1282	Colonies	1461, 1995	Consumption	3276
Classical antiquities	1774	Colonization, African	1462	Contagion	3268
education	1509	Color (optically)	2633	Contracts, law of	1353
mythology	1809	" (painting)	4350	Conundrums	5751
schools	1591	Colors (manufacturing)	3868	Convents	617, 620
Classics, Greek	4627	Combustion	2635	Conversation	5743
Latin	4628	Comedy, see Drama.		Conversion	878
Classification of knowledge	1202	Comets	2693	Cookery	4254
Clergy, lives of	2509–10	Comic works, poetry	5568	Coolie traffic	1463
Climate (hygiene)	3381	prose	5752–3	Co-operation	1471
Climatology	2719	Commentaries, Bible	513–83	Copper	3816
Clinics	3271	" law	1324	Copper engraving	4410
Clocks and watches	3912	Commerce	1628–1750	Coptic language	4831–5
Clothes-making	3904	history of	1630–2	Copts	2243
Clothing (costume)	1841	Commercial dictionaries	1628	Copyright	1368
Clubs (social, etc.)	1836	law	1355	international	1368
Coal, coal mining	3811	periodicals	1629	Corals	2936
Coal oil	3812	Common law	1353	Corea	2138
Coast survey	1755	Common schools	1505–7, 1585	Corn laws	1468–9
Coats of arms	1833	Communication	1633	Cornices	3580, 3607
Cochin China	2125	Communion (Eucharist)	928	Coroners	1400
Codes	1360	Communism	1437	Corporal punishment	1504
Co-education of sexes	1513	Comparative anatomy	2927	Corporations	1634
Coffee	4040	mythology	1807	mining	1635
Coinage	1688	philology	4710	railroad	1636
Coins	1835	Compass	2711, 3755	Correction, houses of	1411

Correlation of forces	2628	Cryptogamia	3105	Devil	886
Correspondence (letter writing)	5737	Crystallography	2758	Devotional theology	961–4
		Cuba	2301	Dew	2719
Swedenborgian	702	Cuneiform languages	4728–32	Dialectics	1208
Corsica	2060	Currency	1688	Dialects, *see* names of languages.	
Cosmetics	4205	Customs and duties	1467		
Cosmogony	1222	Customs and manners	1838–72	Dialogues	5743
Cosmology	2715	Cutaneous diseases	3280	Diamonds	2759
Cossacks	2052–3	Cutlery	3922	Dictionaries, *see* names of languages and subjects.	
Costa Rica	2306	Cyclopedias	5951		
Costumes	1841	Cypher writing	5544	Didactic theology	851–920
Cottages	3582			Die-making	3922
Cotton culture	4038	Daguerreotype	3921	Diet	3240
manufacture	3880	Dairy	4145	Differential calculus	2601
Councils, church	616, 618	Dalmatia	2035–6	Digestion	3217
Counterfeiting	1688	Dancing	4539	Digests	1362
Courts-martial	1358	Danish language	4924–33	Dining	4254
Courts of law	1354	literature	4659	Diphtheria	3276
Cousin's philosophy	1113	Dark ages	1955	Diplomacy	1325
Covenanters	635	Darwinism	2824	Diplomatics	1334
Cows	4144–5	Deaf and dumb education	1603	Directories	2344
Cranberries	4040	institutions	1603	Discipline (education)	1504
Craniology	1278	Deafness	3275	Discovery, history of	1762
Crayon drawing	4396	Death (physiology)	3217	Diseases	3273–3379
Creation	1222	Death (religion)	884	Disinfection	1405
Credit	1697	Death penalty	1414–15	Dispensatories	3271
Creeds	854	Debating societies	1517	Dissection	3216
Cremation	1840	Debt, public	1467	Dissenters	631
Crete	2060	Declamation	5721–35	Distillation	3872
Cricket	4540	Decorative art	4401–6	District of Columbia	2364
Crimea	2053	Deductive logic	1208	Divination	819
Crimean war	2054	Deism	860–1	Diving-bells, diving	3548
Crimes and punishments	1413	Delaware	2362	Divorce	1439
Criminal law	1357	Delusions	1284	Doctrinal history	852
trials	1365	Democracy	1396	theology	851–920
Criminals, juvenile	1412	Demonology	886–7	Dogs	4151
lives of	2511–12	Denmark	2048	Domestic animals	4141–52
Critical science	5554–60	Denominations, religious	618–700	architecture	3582
Criticism, art	5559			arts	4253–80
biblical	512–84	Dentistry	3419	economy	4253
dramatic	5558	Depravity	879	medicine	3268
literary	5556	Derangement, mental	3279	trade	1631
musical	5560	Descartes' philosophy	1103	worship	926
poetical	5557	Descriptive astronomy	2693	Dominoes	4571
Croatia	2035–6	Descriptive geometry	2599	Drainage, agricultural	4029
Crochet	4256	Design (art)	4396	of cities	3662
Croquet	4541	Design, decorative	4401	Drama, criticism of	5558
Croup	3277	Despotism	1395	history of	4622
Cruelty to animals	1409	Detectives	1402	single plays	5603
Crusades	1957	Deuteronomy	516	Dramatic amusements	5601, 5607
Crustacea	2984	Development theory	2824	biography	2513–14

music	4470	Ecclesiology	3581	selections for	1558
Draughts	4571	Echinoderms	2935	Eloquence	5721
Drawing, architectural	3580	Eclectic medicine	3383	Emancipation	1465
free-hand	4397	Eclecticism (philosophy)	1113	Embalming	3216
mathematical	4399	Eclipses	2694	Embargo	1325
mechanical	4399	Economy, domestic	4253	Emblems	1832
perspective	4398	political	1466–1500	Embryology	2821
Drawing books	4396	Ecuador	2310	Emigration	1460
Dreams	1282	Edinburgh	2001–3	Emotions	1224
Dress	1841, 4255	Education	1501–1627	Enamel painting	4350
making	3904	adult	1518	Encaustic "	4350
Driving	4537	art	1512	Encyclopedias, general	5951
Drugs	3270	business	1600	Engineering	3539–71
Druids	718	classical	1509	canal	3546
Druses	718	elementary	1565	civil	3541
Dublin	2001–6	encyclopedias	1501	dictionaries	3539
Dueling	1842	higher	1505	field books	3550
Dutch language	4914–23	history of	1503	harbor	3546
literature	4659	home	1514	hydraulic	3547
painting	4363	institutions	1585–1627	instruments	3550
poetry	5577	legal	1594	mechanical	3542
Reformed Church	641	medical	1595	military	3730
Republic	2041	methods	1521	mining	3810
Duties (morals)	1286	military	1599	periodicals	3540
(commerce)	1467–9	natural science	1597	railroad	3545
Dwarfs	2823	periodicals	1502	steam	3544
Dyeing	3868	philological	1509	topographical	3543
Dynamical electricity	2636	primary	1505	transactions	3540
geology	2735	public documents	1505	England, geography	1999
Dynamics	2629	scientific	1510	history	1984–99
Dysentery	3280	secondary	1505	travels	1999
Dyspepsia	3280	self	1515	English army	1996
		systems of	1521–53	biography	2444
Ear, diseases	3275	of teachers	1519	church	630
functions	3217	text-books	1554–61	dialects	5033
Earth	2715–36	theological	1596	dictionaries	5030
astronomically	2693	treatises on	1504	dissent	631
figure of	2712	Egypt, ancient	1874	drama	5602–6
geographically	1753	modern	2243–4	etymology	5029
Earthquakes	2717	Egyptian language	4831–5	government	1330
East, travels in	2101	literature	4629	grammar	5027
East Indies	2120	Election sermons, see names		language	5026–33
Easter	925	of states.		literature	4652
Eastern churches	616	Elections	1397	navy	1996
empires	1875	Elective franchise	1397	orthography	5028
poetry	5584–90	Electric light	2637	painting	4384–93
states	2345–6	Electricity	2636	philology	5026–33
Eccentrics, lives of	2515–16	Electro-magnetism	2638	philosophy	1117
Ecclesiastical history	612–700	Elementary education	1565	poetry	5561–70
polity	921–60	Elgin marbles	4348	prosody	5032
trials	923	Elocution	5536	sculpture	4348

synonyms	5081	Excise	1467	religious	968
Engraving	4408–12	Exegesis, Biblical	513–83	Field books, engineering	3550
Enigmas	5751	Exhibitions, art	4413	Field sports	4542
Entertaining collections	5754	industrial	3806	Figure of the earth	2712
Entertainments	4532	international	3538	Fiji	2282
Enthusiasm	1224	Exodus	516	Filibusters	2301, 2306
Entomology	2934	Experimental chemistry	2796–8	Final causes	1221
Entozoa	2934	Explorations, ocean	1758	Finances	1687–9
Epics, *see* Poetry.		Explosives	3922	public	1467
Epicureanism	1043	Express companies	1637	Fine arts	4281–4463
Epidemics	3280	Extravagances, religious	820	criticism	5559
Epigrams	5570	Eye, diseases	3275	history	4285
Episcopalianism	630, 636	structure and functions	3216	periodicals	4282
Epistles, Bible	515			Finland	2052–3
Epitaphs	2568	Fables	5696	Finnish language	5006–15
Equity	1353	Facetiæ	5750	literature	4659
Erse language	4945–54	Fairs, agricultural	4153	Fire arms	3718
literature	4659	commercial	1632	departments	1403
poetry	5575	industrial	3806	engines	1403
Eschatology	882–7	Fairy tales	5697	insurance	1694
Esquimaux	2288	Faith	881	works	3922
Essays, miscellaneous	5738	Family	1439	worshippers	717
on subjects; *see* their names.		medicine	3268	Fisheries	4150
Etching	4411	worship	961	Fishes, paleontology	2734
Eternal punishment	887	Fanaticism	820	zoology	2932
Etherization	3420	Farces	5602–3	Fishing	4545
Ethics	1285–1320	Farming	4023–47	tackle	4545
applied	1288–95	Farriery	4148	Flags	1842
Christian	967	Farther India	2121	Flanders	2043
history of	1285	Fashion	4255	Flax	4040
medical	3523	Fasts	925	Flemish painting	4362
systems of	1286	Fatalism	880	Flies	2934
Ethiopia	2246–7	Fathers of the church	615	Flora, local	3005
Ethiopic language	4836–40	Fauna, local	2826	Florence	2025–6
literature	4659	Feasts, church	925	Florida	2369
Ethnology, Ethnography	1771	Federalism	1396	Flower garden	4032
Etiquette	1838	Feet	3216	Flowers	4032
Etruria	1899	Female education	1511	Fluxions	2601
Etymology, comparative	4710	employments	1438	Folk-lore	1807–31
see names of languages.		seminaries	1511	Food (cookery)	4254
Eucharist	928	suffrage	1398–9	(medical)	3240
Europe, generally	1980–83	Fencing	4535	Force and energy	2628
geography	1980	Fermentation	3872	Foreign missions	934–5
history	1981	Ferns	3105	Forgery	1353
statistics	1982	Festivals, church	925	Form books, legal	1364
travels	1983	Fetichism	718	Formation of character	1287
Evidence (law)	1359	Feudal institutions	1956	Formosa	2134–5
Evidence of Christianity	866	Fevers	3280	Forms and precedents	1364
Evil	879, 886	Fichte, philosophy of	1111	Fortification	3731
Evolution	2824	Fiction	5665–5720	Fortune-telling	819
Exchange	1689	history of	4624	Fossils	2734

Founderies	3813	Galleries of art	4412	empire, new	2034
Foundling hospitals	1409	Galvanism	2638	fiction	5668
Fountains	3664	Gambling	1289	government	1395
Fourierism	1436	Game laws	1369	language	4904–13
Fowling	4543	Games	4532, 4546–4620	literature	4655
Fowls	4147	table and parlor	4546	music	4466
Fractures	3416	Gardening	4032–3	painting	4364–73
France	2008–20	flower	4032	philosophy	1108–12
geography	2019	kitchen	4033	poetry	5576
history	3008–18	landscape	4140	reformation	627
travels	2019	market	4033	sculpture	4348
Franchise	1397	window	4032	Germany, geography	2031
Franciscans	620	Gases	2793	history	2030, 2034
Franconia	2030	Gas-fitting	3916	travels	2032
Franco-Prussian war	2017	lighting	3916	Ghosts	1284
Fraud	1355	making	3916	Giants	2823
Free-hand drawing	4397	Gastronomy	4254	Gipsies	2061
Freemasonry	1441	Gauging	3922	Girondists	2012
Free trade	1469	Gazetteers, general	1751	Glaciers	2617
Freewill	880	of countries; see their		Glass	3873
French biography	2446	names.		painting	4407
dictionaries	5039	Gem engraving	4348	Glazing (pottery)	3874
drama	5608	Gems (mineralogy)	2759	Glees	4468, 4473
fiction	5667	sculptured	4348	Globes, use of	1754
government	1395	Genealogy	2566	Glossaries, see names of	
grammar	5036	Generation, spontaneous	2824	languages.	
language	5034–43	Genesis	516	Gloves	3922
literature	4654	Genoa	2025–6	Gnostics	853
painting	4874–86	Geodesy	2712	God	873–4
philosophy	1113–14	Geography of separate		Gold	3816
poetry	5580	countries, etc., see their		Goniometry	2758
revolution	2012	names.		Good Friday	925
sculpture	4348	ancient	1756	Gospels, harmonies of	508
Fresco painting	4350	Biblical	588	Gothic architecture	3580–1
Friction	2629	historical	1753	Goths	1902, 1955
Friendly societies	1475	modern	1753	Gout	3280
Friends, Society of	643	periodicals	1752	Government	1395
Friendship	1295	physical	2716	Grace	877
Fruit culture	4084	school-books	1556	Grafting	4034
Fuel	3914	universal	1753	Grains	4040
Funds and funding	1467	Geology	2731–89	Grammar, comparative	5532
Funeral sermons, see under		and religion	865	general	5532
Biography.		dynamical	2735	of separate languages,	
Funerals	1840	local	2736	see their names.	
Furniture	3909	periodicals and transac-		Grammars (school-books)	1561
Future punishment	887	tions	2732	Granada	2021
Future state	885–7	Geometry	2599	Grangers	1471
		Georgia	2368	Grape culture	4085
Gaelic language	4935–44	German army	3715	Grasses	4040
literature	4659	biography	2446	ornamental	4032
poetry	5575	drama	5609	Gravestones	1840

Graveyards	1840	Heat	2635	travels	2109
Gravel (disease)	3280	Heathen religions	707–817	Home education	1514
Gravitation	2629	Heating	3914	missions	936
Great Britain	1984–2000	Heaven	885	Homicide	1413–15
Greece, ancient	1898	Hebrew history	1897	Homiletics	932
modern, geography	2059	language	4713–17	Homeopathy	3382
history	2058	literature	4649	Honey	4148
travels	2059	poetry	5586	Horned cattle	4144
Greek antiquities	1774	Hebrides	2001–3	Horse	4143
architecture	3578	Hedges	4040	Horse-racing	4537
church	616	Hegelian philosophy	1110	shoeing	4143
classics	4627	Heliotypes	3921	Horsemanship	4537
language	4484–93	Hell	887	Horticulture	4032
literature	4627	Heraclitic philosophy	7046	Hospitals	3271
mythology	1809	Heraldry	1883	Hotels	1763–4
philosophy	1036–1045	Herbariums	3004	Hothouses	4032
poetry	5571	Heredity	2823	House-keeping	4253
sculpture	4348	Heresies	853	Housewifery	4253
Green-houses	4032	Hermaphrodites	2821	Huguenots	627
Greenland	2289	Hermeneutics, Biblical	584	Human anatomy	3216
Grounds, private	4140	Hermetics	1276	Human body	3216–17
Groves	4089	Herpetology	2931	body and mind	1277
Guatemala	2306	Herzegovina	2056–7	mind	1001–1284
Guiana	2309	Hieroglyphics	4831–5	physiology	3217
Guide-books	1763	Highlands, Scottish	2001–3	Humane societies	1409
Guilds	1472	Highwaymen	2511–12	Humorous works, poetical	5568
Guillotine	1414	Himalayas	2117–18	prose	5750–3
Guinea	2239	Hindoo languages	4749–64	Hungary	2039–40
Gun-cotton	3922	literature	4649	Hunting	4543
Gun-making	3907	Hindostan	2116–18	Hurricanes	2719
Gunnery	3718	Histology	3216	Husbandry	4023–48
Gunpowder	3922	Historical books of Bible		Hybridism	2824
Guns, sporting	4543		507, 514	Hydraulic engineering	3547
Gutta percha	3901	charts and tables	1769	Hydraulics	2630
Gymnastics	4534	collaterals	1769–1872	Hydrodynamics	2630
Gypsies	2061	geography	1753, 1756	Hydrography	1755
		theology	851–4	Hydromechanics	2630
Habeas corpus	1853	History of subjects and countries, see their names.		Hydropathy	3380
Hair	3217			Hydrophobia	3280
Hamiltonian philosophy	1107	ancient	1873	Hydrostatics	2630
Hand	3216	ecclesiastical	611–700	Hygiene	3238–65
Harbors	3546	modern	1979, 1981	Hymnology	964
Harmony, music	4467	philosophy of	1766	Hypochondria	3280
of gospels	508	universal	1768		
Harness-making	3902	Histrionics	5601	Icebergs	1759–60
Hasheesh	3242	Holland: geography	2042	Iceland	2049
Hats	3904	history	2041	Icelandic language	4924–33
Health	3238–65	travels	2042	literature	4659
public	1405	Holy Ghost	878	poetry	5579
resorts	3381	Holy land: geography	588	Ichnology	2734
Heart diseases	3280	history	1897, 2108	Ichthyology	2932

Idiocy	1605	Instruments, engineering	3550	Israelites, *see* Jews.	
Idiot schools	1605	making	3913	Italian drama	5612
Idolatry	707–817	Insurance	1692–4	fiction	5669
Illinois	2380	accidental	1692	language	5064–73
Illumination (lighting)	3915	fire	1694	literature	4656
(art)	4406	life	1693	music	4466
Imagination	1225	marine	1694	painting	4351–61
Immersion	929, 930	Integral calculus	2601	philosophy	1119
Immigration	1460	Intellect	1225	poetry	5581
Immortality	885	Intellectual philosophy	1221–75	renaissance	2025
Imprisonment for debt	1353	Intemperance	1290, 3243	sculpture	4348
Incarnation	875–6	Intercommunication	1633	Italy, geography	2026
Incunabula	6156	Interest	1687–9	history	2025
Independents	638	tables	1696	travels	2026
India, *see* Hindostan.		Interior administration	1400		
Indian, *see* Hindoo.		Intermarriage	1439	Jacobins	2012
Indiana	2379	Intermediate state (theol.)		Jainism	708
Indians, American	2287		884–5	Jamaica	2302
ethnology	1771	Interment	1840	Jansenism	619
languages	5074	Internal improvements	1400	Japan	2184–5
India-rubber	3901	International copyright	1368	Japanese art	4295
Indigestion	3240	exhibitions	3538	language	4470–4
Indoor amusements	4546–4620	law	1325	literature	4649
Induction	1203	Intolerance	613	Japanning	3922
Inductive logic	1203	Inventions	3809	Java	2128
Industrial drawing	4399	Inventors, lives of	2521–2	Jerusalem	2103
exhibitions	3538, 3806	Invertebrates, paleontol-		Jests	5750
history	3807	ogy	2734	Jesuit missions	934
schools	1601, 1598	zoology	2938	Jesuits	621
Inebriate institutions	3248	Investments	1689	Jesus, *see* Christ.	
Infanticide	1357, 1413	Ionian Islands	2058–9	Jewelry	3922
Infantry	3716–17	Ionic philosophy	1036	Jewish literature	4649
Infidelity	858–863	Iowa	2382	philosophy	1005
Infidel books	860	Iranian languages	4743–7	religion	705
Inoculation	3280	literature	4649	Jews, ancient	1897
Inorganic chemistry	2794	Ireland, geography	2005	medieval	1958
Inquisition	622	history	2004	modern	1958
Insane hospitals	3279	travels	2006	John, epistles of	516
Insanity	3279	Irish church	614	gospel of	516
Inscriptions	1773	language	4945–54	revelation of	516
Insects	2934	literature	4659	Joinery	3609
Inspiration of Bible	867–8	music	4466	Journalism	4625
Instinct	2825	poetry	5565	Journeys round the world	1757
Institutions, educational		Iron, architecture	3663	Judaism	705
	1585–1627	bridges	3612	Judges, lives of	2519–20
political	1395–1433	manufacture	3816	Judgment and future state	885
religious	921–960	metallurgy	3814	Jugglery	4591
social	1484–1500	mining	3810	Jurisprudence	1324
Instruction	1521–53	ships	3754	medical	3521
Instrumental music		Iron-clad ships	3754	Jury trial	1353
	4472, 75–4530	Irrigation	4153	Justification by faith	881

Juvenile books	5698	of nations	1325	history of	4621–4708
criminals	1412	of real property	1354	medieval	4650
		Roman	1327	modern	4651
Kabbala	705	of U. S.	1331	oriental	4649
Kafirs	2241	Lawns	4140	Lithography	4413
Kaleidoscope	2633	Lawyers, lives of	2519–20	Lithology	2747
Kamtschatka	2187	Lead, metallurgy of	3816	Liturgies	962
Kansas	2385	mining	3810	Locke's philosophy	1105
Kant, philosophy of	1109	Leather	3902–3	Lock-making	3906
Keltic languages	4934–64	Lectures	5739	Locomotives	3545
literature	4659	Legends	5697	Logarithms	2604
Kentucky	2376	Legerdemain	4591	Logic	1203
Kindergarten	1588	Legislation	1400	Lollards	613
Kinematics	2629	Legitimacy	1395	London	2000
Kings, lives of	2533–4	Lent	925	Longevity	3217
Kitchen economy	4254	Lepidoptera	2934	Lord's supper	928
gardening	4053	Lettering, ornamental	4495	Lorraine	2008
Knighthood	1956	Letter writing	4405	Lotteries	1289
Koran	706	Letters, alphabetical	5533	Louisiana	2372
		(correspondence)	5737	Love	1224
Labor questions	1470–3	Levant	2102	Low Countries	2041–2
Labrador	2290–1	Leveling	3549	Luke, gospel of	516
Lace-making	4257	Leviticus	516	Lunacy	3279
Laconics	5744–5	Lexicons, see names of lan-		Lunatic asylums	3279
Lamaism	710	guages.		Lung diseases	3276
Land surveying	3549	Libel	1369	Lutheranism	628
Landlord and tenant	1354	Liberia	2239		
Landscape gardening	4140	Liberty	1395	Macaronics	5573
Language	4709–5553	of press	4625	Machine engraving	4408
universal	5531	Libraries, sales of	6269	Machinery	3808
Lapland	2044	Library catalogues	6363–84	Madagascar	2255
Late war (1812)	2332	economy	6361	Madeira	2253
Latin classics	4627–8	history and reports	6321–62	Madness	3279
language	4894–4903	Lichens	3105	Magazines	5801
literature	4628	Life (future)	885	Magic	819
poets	5572	(physiologically)	3217	Magnetism	2638
Laundry	3922	Life insurance	1698	animal	1283
Law, ancient	1326	Light	2633	Magyar language	4996–5005
canon	1328	Lighthouses and ships	3759	literature	4659
civil	1327	Lightning	2636	poetry	5591
commercial	1355	Lights and fuel	3914	Magyars	2039–40
common	1353	Line engraving	4410	Mahometanism, see Moham—	
constitutional	1329–52	Linen manufacture	3881	Mails	1404
criminal	1357	Linguistics	5531–53	Maine	2350
dictionaries of	1321	Liquors	3872	Malacca	2127
English	1330	Litany	962	Malaria	3246
French	1332	Literary criticism	5554–8	Malay language	4775
history of	1323	Literary men, lives of	2503–4	Malaysia	2127
maritime	1356	property	1368	Malt	3872
mercantile	1355	Literature, ancient	4626	Malta	2060
military	1358	classical	4627–8	Mamelukes	2243

Mammalia (paleontology)	2734	
(zoology)	2929	
Man, mental nature of	1221–1280	
ethnology	1771	
natural history of	2828	
physiology of	3217	
Mania, maniacs	3279	
Manners and customs	1836–72	
Manuals, collectors'	2989	
travelers'	1764	
Manufactures	3877	
history of	3807	
Manures	4030	
Manuscripts	6055	
Maps	1754	
astronomical	2694	
Marble manufacture	3922	
Marbles (sculpture)	4848	
Marine architecture	3753	
insurance	1694	
law	1356	
Maritime law	1356	
Mark, gospel of	516	
Market gardening	4033	
Marriage, customs	1839	
ethics	1292	
Martial law	1358	
Martyrs	613	
Maryland	2363	
Masonry	3608	
" Free	1441	
Massachusetts	2353	
Materia medica	3270	
Materialism	860–1	
Materials, building	3607	
Maternity	3418	
Mathematical drawing	4399	
instruments	3550	
tables	2604	
Mathematics	2594–2624	
history of	2594	
periodicals and transactions	2595	
Matthew, gospel of	516	
Mauritius	2276	
Mausoleums	1840	
Maxims	5745	
Measles	3277	
Measures and weights	1690–1	
Mechanic arts and trades	3801–4022	
dictionaries	3801	
exhibitions	3806	
periodicals and transactions	3802	
Mechanical drawing	4399	
engineering	3542	
Mechanics' associations	1472	
Mechanics' science	2629	
" molecular	2639	
" lives of	2521–2	
Medals	1835	
Medieval art	4292	
history	1955	
literature	4650	
manners and customs	1955	
philosophy	1072	
sculpture	4348	
Medical biography	2527–8	
botany	3205	
dictionaries	3211	
education	1595	
ethics	3523	
history	3213	
jurisprudence	3521	
periodicals and transactions	3212	
practice	3266–3415	
schools	1595	
Medicine	3211–3533	
veterinary	4142	
Meditations, religious	963	
Mediterranean	2060	
Melancholy	3279	
Melodeon	4481	
Melody	4467	
Memoirs, see Biography.		
Memory	1225	
Mensuration	3549	
Mental derangement	3279	
faculties	1224–75	
hygiene	3279	
philosophy	1001–1284	
science	1001–1320	
Mercantile law	1355	
manuals	1696	
theory and practice	1697	
Merchants, lives of	2505–6	
Mesmerism	1283	
Mesopotamia	2114	
Messiah	875–6	
Metal manufactures	3813	
Metallurgy	3814	
Metaphysics	1001–1275	
Meteorology	2719	
Methodism	639	
Methodology	1201	
Methods of education	1501–1584	
Metric system	1691	
Metrology	1690–1	
Mexican war	2333	
Mexico, geography	2305	
history	2304	
travels	2305	
Mezzotint	4410	
Michigan	2378	
Microscopy	2937	
Middle Ages	1955–78	
Middle States	2357–62	
Midwifery	3418	
Military arts	3713–51	
engineering	3730	
history	3715	
law	1358	
schools	1599	
Militia	3715	
Milk	4145	
Millennium	888	
Millinery	4255	
Mills, cotton, woolen, etc.	3878–80	
paper	3877	
Mill-work, mill-wrights	3877	
Mind, science of	1001–1275	
Mind and body	1277	
Mineral waters	3381	
Mineralogy	2747	
Mines, mining	3810	
Mining corporations	1635	
Miniatures	4350	
Ministers of the gospel, lives of	2509–10	
office and duty of	931	
Minnesingers	5576	
Minnesota	2384	
Miracles	871–2	
Missions	933–6	
Protestant, foreign	935	
" home	936	
Romanist	934	
Mississippi river	2341–2	
State	2371	
valley	2341–2	
Missouri river	2341–2	

State	2381	Municipal government	1395	Nebraska	2385
Mnemonics	5539	Murder	1357, 1413–15	Necromancers	819
Modeling (sculpture)	4348	Mutual aid societies	1471	Needle-work	4256
Modern architecture	3580	Music	4464–4580	Negro slavery	1462–5
history	1979	criticism	5560	Neo-platonism	1042
Mohammedanism	706	dictionaries	4464	Nervous system	3216
Molecular mechanics	2639	history	4466	Nestorians	616
Mollusca (paleontology)	2734	periodicals	4465	Netherlands	2041–2
(zoology)	2935	sacred	4469, 4471	Neuroptera	2934
Monarchy	1395	secular	4468	Neutrals, law of	1356
Monachism, monasteries,		single compositions	4472	Nevada	2387
monastic orders	617, 620	songs with	4473	New Brunswick	2296–7
Money	1687–8	vocal	4473–4	England	2345–6
Mongolian language	4985	Musical collections	4468–9	Newfoundland	2298
Mongols	2105	Musical composition	4467	Granada	2306
Monks	617, 620	Musical instruments	4475–4580	Guinea	2130
Monitors, iron-clads	3754	Musicians, lives of	2523–4	Hampshire	2351
Monograms	4495	Mysteries, ancient	718	Jersey	2359
Monopolies	1630	Mysticism	701	Mexico	2386
Montana	2390	Mythology, comparative	1807	Platonism	1042
Montenegro	2056–7	classical	1809	Testament	506, 515
Monuments, sepulchral	1840	German	1811	New York, city	2358
Moon	2693	Oriental	1808	State	2357
Moral philosophy, history	1285	Scandinavian	1810	Newspapers	5851
systems	1286	Myths	1807	New Zealand	2279
Morals of amusements	1289			Nicaragua	2306
business	1291	Names	2569–70	Nile	2245
marriage	1292	Naples	2025–6	Nineveh	1876
politics	1288	Napoleon I	2013	Nobility	1833
society	1295	Narcotics	3242	Nobles, lives of	2533–4
young men	1293	National costumes	1841	Non-Christian religions	702–817
young women	1294	customs	1836–72	Normal schools	1519, 1601
Moravians	642	Natural history	2820–3210	Norman conquest	1988
Moravian missions	933	Biblical	589	Normandy	2008, 2019
Morea	2058–9	philosophy	2625–2690	Norse language	4924–33
Mormonism	704	science	2691–3210	literature	4659
Morocco	2250	selection	2824	poetry	5579
Morphology	2820	system of botany	3003–4	Norsemen	2044
Mortar (building)	3876	theology	855	North Africa	2248–50
(ordnance)	3718	Naturalization	1460	North America, ethnology	1771
Mortality statistics	1693	Nature	2591–3210	geography	2283
Mortgages	1354	Naval architecture	3753	history	2283
Mosaics	4350	Naval arts	3752–3800	travels	2284
Moslems	706	Naval men, lives of	2537–8	North Carolina	2366
Mosquito Shore	2306	Naval schools	1599	Northmen	2044
Mosses	3105	Naval war	3757	Norway	2046
Mothers (home education)	1514	Navies	3752	Nosology	3268
Moths	2934	Navigation	2711	Nova Scotia	2294–5
Mound-builders	1772	laws	1355	Novels	5665–95
Mountains	2716	Navy, British	1996	Nubia	2240
Mulberry	4037	U. S.	2338	Numbers, book of	516

Numismatics	1835	Ornithology	2930	Parseeism, Parsees	717
Nunneries	617, 620	Orphans, orphan asylums	1409	Parthia	1875
Nursery	1514	Orthoepy, *see* names of languages.		Partnership	1355
Nursing	3272			Parturition	3418
		Orthography, *see* under names of languages.		Passions	1225–75
Oaths	1824			Pastel drawing	4350
Object teaching	1521	Osteology	2937, 3216	Pastoral theology	931
Observations, astronomical	2693	Ottoman empire, geography	2057	Patagonia	2317
Obstetrics	3418	history	2056	Patent law	1367
Ocean, exploration	1758	travels	2057	Patents	3809
geography	1755	Out-door sports	4531–45	Pathology	3268
transportation	3752	Oysters	2935	Patriarchal institutions	
Oceanica, ethnology	1771				1395, 1767
geography and travels	2280	Pacific ocean	2280	Patriotism	1288
Odd Fellows	1442	Paganism	707–817	Patristics	615
Odontology	2821	Painters, lives of	2501–2	Patronage	1400
Ohio	2377	Painting	4283, 4349	Pauperism	1410
Oil, animal	3922	color	4283	Pawnbroking	1698
coal	3812	criticisms	5559	Peace reform	1459
manufacture	3922	American	4394	Pears	4034
painting	4350	Dutch	4363	Peat	3914
vegetable	3922	English	4364–93	Pedobaptism	640, 929–30
Old Testament	505, 514	Flemish	4362	Peerage	1833
Ontology	1222	French	4374–83	Peloponnesus	2058–9
Operas	4470	German	4364–73	Penal law	1357
Opium	3245, 1290	Italian	4351–61	Penance	619
Opium trade	1290	landscape	4349	Peninsular war	2022
Optics	2633	materials	4350	Penitentiaries	1411
Oracles	819	methods	4350	Penmanship	5540
Oratorios	4471	Painting (trade)	3922	Pennsylvania	2360
Oratory	5721–35	Paintings, collections	4413	Pentateuch	514
Orcades	2001–3	Palæography	1834	Perception	1225
Orchards	4034	Palæontology	2734	Perfectionists	646
Orders of architecture	3574	Palestine	588, 2103–4	Perfumery	3870
Ordinances, religious	926	Palmistry	819	Periodicals, *see* names of subjects.	
Ordination sermons	931	Panama	2306		
Ordnance	3718	Pantheism	862–3	Perpetual motion	2629
Oregon	2390	Papacy	618–23	Persecutions	613
Organ	4479–80	Paper-hanging	3922	Persia, ancient	1877
Organic chemistry	2795	Paper manufacture	3922	modern	2109–10
remains	2734	Paper money	1687–8, 1467	Persian language	4743–7
Oriental architecture	3576	Papua	2130	literature	4649
churches	616	Paraguay	2316	poetry	5585
languages	4711–4800	Parchment	3922	Personal liberty	1329–52
philosophy	1005	Parent and child	1353	property	1355
poetry	5584–90	Paris	2020	rights	1324
Origin of language	4710	Parks, public	1407	Perspective	4398
Origin of species	2824	Parliament	1984, 1400	Peru	2311
Orkneys	2001–3	Parliamentary law	1401	Pests, agricultural	4031
Ornamental design	4401	Parodies	5568, 5753	Petrifaction	2738
work	4256–80	Parrots	4152	Petroleum	3812

Pharmacopœias	3270	Piracy	1356–7	Polyglot Bibles	1
Pharmacy	3270–1	Pisciculture	4149	Polygraphy	5736
Philippine Islands	2130	Plague	3280	Polynesia	2280
Philology	4709–5530	Planets	2693	languages	4801
Philosophers, lives of	2525–6	Plans for building	3607	Polyps	2936
Philosophy	1001–1320	Plants, *see* Botany, 3001–		Polytheism	707–817
ancient	1004	3210; *also* Agricul-		Pomology	4034
history of	1003–1200	ture.		Poor	1409–10
mental	1001–1284	Platonic philosophy	1039	Poor laws	1410
modern	1102–1200	Platonists, new	1042	Popery	618–23
moral	1285–1320	Playing-cards	4549–70	Popes, lives of	618, 2509–10
natural	2625–90	Plays, *see* Drama	5602–64	Population	1466
of art	4288	Pleading	1353	Porcelain	3874
history	1766	Plumbing	3662	Portrait painting	4349
language	4710	Plurality of worlds	2693	Portraits, photographic	3921
literature	5556	Pneumatics	2631	Portugal	2024
religion	856	Pneumatology	878	Portuguese language	5054–63
sociology	1767, 1435	Poetical books of Bible	516	literature	4658
Phœnicia	1905	Poetical works, complete	5569	poetry	5583
Phœnician language	4712	Poetry	5561–6000	Positivism	1115
Phonetic short-hand	5541	American	5566–7	Postage-stamps	1404
spelling	5543	collections of	5561–7	Post-offices	1404
Phonography	5541	criticism of	5557	Potato	4040
Phonology	5531	French	5580	Pottery	3874
Photography	3921	German	5576	Poultry	4147
Photo-lithography	3921	Greek	5571	Powder	3922
Phrenology	1278	history of	4623	Prayer	961
books against	1279	humorous	5568	Prayer-books	962
Phthisis	3276	Italian	5581	Prayer-meetings	961
Physical education	3241, 4533–9	Latin	5572	Preachers, lives of	2509–10
geography	2716	Oriental	5584–90	Preaching	932
Physicians, lives of	2527–8	sacred	964	Precedence	1833
Physics	2625–90	satirical	5568	Precedents, legal	1364
dictionaries and encyclo-		Spanish	5582	Precious metals	3816
pedias	2625	Portuguese	5583	Precious stones	2759
molecular	2639	Poets, lives of	2529–30	Predestination	880
periodicals and transac-		Poisons	3522	Pregnancy	3418
tions	2626	Poland, history	2050	Pre-historic archæology	1772
Physiognomy	1281	travels	2051	Presbyterianism	637
Physiography	2716	Polar regions	1759–60	Prescriptions	3270
Physiology	3217	Polemic theology	851–920	Press, liberty of	4621
comparative	2821	Police	1402	Prices, history of	1630
mental	1277	Polish language	4965	Primeval man	1772
vegetable	3004	literature	4651	Primitive Christianity	614
Pianoforte	4475–6	Politeness	1295, 1838	Primogeniture	1354
Picts	2001	Political economy	1466–1500	Printing	3917
Picture galleries	4412	institutions	1395	Prints, books of	4412
Piedmont	2025–6	science	1395–1500	Prison associations	1411
Pig	4153	speeches	5724	Prisons	1411
Pigeons	4153	Politics, morals of	1288	Private theatricals	5607
Pigmies	2823	Polygamy	1357	Private worship	961

Privateers	1325, 1356	Pulpit oratory	932	Reform schools	1607
Probabilities	2603	Pumps	2630	Reformation	627
Production	1466	Punctuation	5027	Reformatory associations	
Productions of the soil	4028–4189	Punishment	1413–15	and institutions	1411
		Punjaub	2116–18	Reformed church	641
Professional education	1593–1601	Puritans	632	Regeneration	878
		Puseyism	633	Regimen	3239
Prohibited books	6055	Puzzles	5751	Registration	1416
Prohibition	1290	Pygmies	2823	Regulations, army	3716
Projectiles	3718	Pyramids	1874	navy	3757
Promissory notes	1355	Pyrites	2747	Religion and philosophy	864
Pronunciation	5536	Pyrotechnics	3922	and science	865
Property	1466, 1470	Pyrrhonism	1041	history of	611
Property law	1354–5	Pythagoreanism	1037	philosophy of	856
tax	1467			practical	965–90
Prophecy	869–70	Quadrumana	2929	Religions, non-Christian	702–817
Prophetical books of Bible	514, 516	Quadrupeds	2929	Religious anecdotes	969
		Quakers	643	associations	933–60
Prose composition, English	5534	Qualitative analysis	2797	biography	2507–10
Prosody, see names of languages.		Quantitative "	2798	ceremonies	925
Prostitution	1406	Quarantine	1405	charities	940
Protection	1468	Quarrying	3810	education	1596
Protestant episcopal church	636	Quaternions	2602	encyclopedias	585, 851, 991
Protestant reformation	627	Queens, lives of	2533–4	essays	996
Protestantism	626	Quotations	5742	fiction	968
Protoplasm	2824			institutions	921–60
Protozoa	2936	Race-horse	4143	orders	617, 620
Provençal language	5043	Races of man	1771	periodicals	992
literature	4654	Racing	4537	philosophy	864
Proverbs	5744	Radiates, (paleontology)	2734	superstitions	820
Book of	516	(zoology)	2936	Renaissance	1981
Providence	873	Railroad corporations	1636	Rent	1466
Provincialisms	5033	engineering	3545	Repentance	877
Pruning	4034, 4039	locomotives	3545	Reptiles (paleontology)	2734
Prussia	2033	transportation	1633	(zoology)	2931
Psalms	516	Railways, laws of	1355	Republicanism	1396
Pseudonyms	6055	Rain	2719	Resistance of materials	3541
Psychology	1224	Rank	1833	Resurrection	884
Public accounts	1467	Rationalism	860–1	Retribution	887
administration	1395–1433	Readers (school books)	1558	Revealed religion	866
charities	1409	Reading, art of	5536	Revelation, Book of	516
documents, see names of states, countries, etc.		Reading clubs	1516	Revenue	1467
		Reading, courses	1516	Reviews	5801
education	1505–7, 1585	for self-education	1515	Revivals	965
finance	1467	Real estate law	1354	Revolution, American	2331
health	1405	Reason	1203	English	1991
houses	1402	Rebellion, Southern	2335	French	2012
lands	1467	Rebuses	5751	Rhetoric	5537
schools	1505–7, 1585	Receipt or recipe books	4254	sacred	932
speaking	5721–35	Recreations	4531–4620	Rhode Island	2355
worship	925–6	Redemption	877	Riddles	5751

Riding	4537	Rural sports	4542-5	Scholastic philosophy	1072
Right of search	1325	Russia, geography	2053	School and church	1520
Rights and liberties	1329-52	history	2052	School apparatus	1564
Riots	1402	language	4965	architecture	1562
Rites and ceremonies	925	literature	4659	Schools, art	1512
Ritualism	633	poetry	5578	Bible in	1520
River transportation	1638	travels	2053	common	1585
Rivers (engineering)	3547			evening	1585
Roads, common	3552	Sabbatarians	927	grammar	1590
Rocky Mountains	2341	Sabbath	927	high	1590
Rodentia	2929	reform	927	industrial	1602
Roman administration	1827	schools	939	law	1594
antiquities	1774	Sacrament of baptism	929-30	medical	1595
architecture	3579	Lord's Supper	928	military	1599
art	4290	Sacraments	926-8	naval	1599
Catholicism	618-623	Sacred art	4291	parochial	1520
empire	1902	biography	2507-10	primary	1587
history, ancient	1900-3	books, see names of religions.		prison	1411
history, modern	2027	history	611-700	private	1586
inquisition	622	music	4469, 4471	professional	1593-9
law	1327	poetry	964	public	1585
literature	4628	rhetoric	932	ragged	1606
mythology	1809	Sacrifices	925	reform	1607
poetry	5572	Saddlery	3902	scientific	1597
sculpture	4348	Sagas	1810	secondary	1589
Romance	5565-95	Sahara	2256	special	1592
criticism of	5556	Sailors, lives of	2537-8	Sunday	939
Romanic languages	5231	St. Domingo	2303	technological	1598
Romanism	618-23	Saints, lives of	2507-10	theological	1596
Romansh language	5231	Sale catalogues of books	6269	Schopenhauer's philosophy	1116
Romantic literature	5565-98	Salt manufacture	3922	Science and religion	865
Rome, church of	618-23	Salvation	877	mental	1001-1284
books against	623	Sandwich Islands	2281	moral	1285-1320
history	618	Sanitary commissions	3404	natural	2591-3210
missions	934	legislation	1405	Scientific education	1508, 1593
theology	619	Sanskrit language	4749-53	institutions	1510, 1597
Rome, city, antiquities	1774	literature	4649	men, lives of	2535-6
history	1903, 2027	Sardinia, island	2060	periodicals and transactions,	
topography	1923, 2027	kingdom	2025-6	see names of subjects.	
Rome, empire	1902	Satan	886	schools	1510, 1597
regal and republican	901	Satire	5753, 5568	societies	2592
Romish church	618-23	Savings banks	1475	See also names of subjects.	
Rope-making	3922	Saxon, see Anglo-Saxon		travels	1758
Rose	4032	Saxony	2030-2	Scotland, history	2001
Rosicrucians	1443	Scandinavia	2044-5	geography	2002
Roumania	2057	Scandinavian language	4924-33	travels	2003
Rowing	4536	literature	4659	Scotch churches	634-5
Royal lives	2533-4	poetry	5579	language	5033
Rubber manufactures	3901	Scepticism	858-61	literature	4659
Ruminants	2929	Schelling's philosophy	1112	music	4466
Rural architecture	3582	Schleswig Holstein	2048	philosophy	1107

poetry	5564	Shipwrecks	8758	Societies, *see* names of subjects or objects.	
Screw propulsion	8756	Shoemaking	3903		
Scripture, *see* Bible.		Shooting	8718, 4542–8	Society	1321–1750
Scrofulous diseases	3280	Short-hand	5541–2	Sociology	1395–1627
Sculptors, lives of	2501–2	Shrubbery	4140	periodicals	1434
Sculpture	4848	Siam	2123	Socratic philosophy	1038
criticism of	5559	Siberia	2137	Soils	4028
Seal engraving	4348	Sicily	2060	Solar system	2693
Seamanship	8755	Sick-room	3272	Soldiers, lives of	2537–8
Secession	2335	Sieges	8715–16	Somnambulism	1282
Second advent	883	Sierra Leone	2239	Songs and ballads, American	5567
Second sight	819	Sight (optics)	2633	English	5562
Secret societies	1440–58	(diseases)	3275	Songs with music	4478
Sects, Christian	628–700	Signals	3919	Sonnets	5563
Select works, selections, extracts	5741	Sign-painting	4495	Sophist philosophy	1038
		Silk culture	4037		
Self-education	1515–16	manufacture	3881	Sorcery	819
Semitic languages	4712–37	worm	4037	Soteriology	875–81
literature	4649	Silver metallurgy	3816	Soudan	2242
poetry	5586	mining	3810	Soul	1224
Sensation	1223	money	1688	Sound	2632
Sense	1223–4	Simony	922	South Africa	2241
Sepulchres	1840	Sin	879	South America	2307
Sepulture	1840	Singing	4474	South Carolina	2367
Sermons	994	Sintooism	716	South Sea	2280
Serpents	2931	Sisters of charity	620	Southern States	2347
Servants	4253	mercy	620	Spain, geography	2023
Servia	2056–7	Skating	4593	history	2021
Service books	962	Skepticism	858–63	travels	2023
Sewerage	3662	Skin diseases	3280	Spanish art	4293
Sewing	4256	Skye	2001–3	dictionaries	5044
Sewing machine	3922	Slander	1358	drama	5610
Sex in education	1513	Slang	5033	fiction	5670
Sexual ethics	1292	Slating	3607	language	5044–53
science	3217	Slavery	1462–5	literature	4657
Shades and shadows	4396	American	1465	music	4466
Shakers	703	England and	1464	poetry	5582
Shakespeare, biographies	2514	Slavic languages	4975–84	Specie payment	1687–8
comments	5605	literature	4659	Species (natural history)	2824
editions	5604	poetry	5578	Specifications for building	3607
Shakesperiana	5606	Sleep	1282	Spectacles (for eyes)	3275
Sheep	4146	Sleep-walking	1282	Specters	1284
Shells	2935	Small-pox	3280	Spectroscope	2634
fossil	2734	Soap-making	3871	Spectrum analysis	2634
Shemitic, *see* Semitic.		Social ethics	1295	Speech, organs of	3216
Shetland islands	2001–3	intercourse	1485	use of, *see* Linguistics, Philology, Oratory.	
Ship-building	8753	organization	1434–1460		
canals	3546	reform	1435–7	Speeches, collections of	5722–3
Shipping and freighting	1633	science	1434–1500	single	5724–5
Shipping laws	1355–6	Socialism	1436	Spencer, philosophy of	1117
Ships	8753			Spherical astronomy	2693

geometry	2599	Stoves	3914	Table-talk	5749
trigonometry	2600	Strategy	3717	Tables, mathematical	2604
Spiders	2934	Strawberries	4040	Tachygraphy	5542
Spinoza, philosophy of	1104	Strength of materials	3541	Tactics	3717
Spiritism or spiritualism	818	Strikes	1478	Tailoring	3904
Spitzbergen	1759	Stringed instruments		Tales, *see* Fiction.	
Spontaneous generation	2824		4475–8, 4471	Talmud	705
Sporting guns	4543	Stuarts	1990	Tanning	3922
Sports and games	4531–4620	Study, methods of		Taouism	712
athletic	4533–41		1521–53, 1515–16	Tapestry	4256
field	4542–5	Stuttering	3280	Tariffs	1468–9
Stables	4143	Sublime and beautiful	5554	Tartary	2136
Stage (dramatic)	5601	Submarine armor	3548	Taste and criticism	5554–60
Stained glass	4407	telegraph	3919	Taxation	1467
Stairbuilding	3610	Suez canal	3546	Taxidermy	2938
Stammering	3280	Suffrage	1397–9	Tea cultivation	4040
Stamps (postal)	1404	Sugar-cane, cultivating	4036	Teachers, education of	
Standing army	3715	Sugar manufacture	4086		1519, 1601
Starch manufacture	3922	Suicide	3279	Teaching	1521–53
Stars	2693	Sumatra	2126	Technical dictionaries, *see* names	
State	1395	Summer-houses	3582	of subjects.	
ethics	1288	Sun	2693	Technology	3805, 3867
papers	1325	Sunday laws	927	Teeth	3419
rights	1331	Sunday-schools	939	Tehuantepec, isthmus	2306
trials	1365	Supernaturalism	857	Telegraphy	3919
Statesmen, lives of	2539–40	Superstition	820	Telephone	3920
Statics	2629	Surgery	3416–3520	Telescope	2693
Statistical methods	1770, 1416	Surnames	2569	Temperaments	1280
Statistics	1770	Surveying	3549	Temperance	1290, 3242
Statuary	4348	Susceptibility	1223	Temperature	2719
Statute law	1361	Sweden	2047	Templars	1443
Steam-engine, steam engineering	3544	language	4924	Tennessee	2375
Steel	3816	literature	4659	Terra cotta	3875
engraving	4410	poetry	5579	Testacea	2931
Stenography	5542	Swedenborgians	702	Testament, New	506, 515
Stereotyping	3917	Swimming	4538	Old	505, 514
Stereoscope	2633	Swine	4153	Testamentary law	1354
Stethoscope	3276	Switzerland, history	2028	Testimony	1359
Stewart's philosophy	1107	travels	2029	Texas	2373
Stills, distilling	3872	Syllogism	1208	Textile fabrics	3878–3900
Stimulants and narcotics	3242	Symbolism	1832	Thanksgiving	925
ethics of using	1290	Synonyms, *see* names of languages.		Theater, *see* Drama	5601–64
Stipple engraving	4410			ethics of	1289
Stock, live	4141	Syphilis	3280	Theaters	5601
Stocks	1689	Syria	2107	Theatricals, private	5607
Stoic philosophy	1044	Syriac language	4733–7	Theft	1357, 1413
Stomach diseases	3280	Systematic botany	3004	Theism	857
Stone-cutting	3922	theology	851–920	Theodicy	877
Stoneware	3874			Theological essays	996
Storms	2719	Tableaux	4593	schools	1596
		Table and parlor games	4546	Theology	851–1000

devotional	961–4	Treason	1357	University education	1592
doctrinal	851–920	Treasury administration	1467	Upholstering	3910
natural	855	Treaties	1325	Uruguay	2315
pastoral	931	Trees, tree culture	4039	Useful arts	3531–4255
practical	965–90	Trees, ornamental	4140	Useful knowledge, collections of	5951–6000
systematic and polemic	851–920	Trespass	1353		
		Trials, civil	1366	Usury	1687–9
Therapeutics	3268	criminal	1365	Utah	2388
Thibet	2133	ecclesiastical	923		
Thirty-nine articles	680	Trigonometry	2600	Van Diemen's Land	2278
Thirty years' war	2030	Trinity	873–4	Vases	3874, 3813
Thomsonianism	3383	Troubadours and trouvères	4654, 5580	Vaudois	625
Thought	1203			Vedas	707
Throat diseases	3276	Trunk-making	3922	Vegetable physiology	3004
Thunder	2719	Trusts, trustees	1353	Vegetables	4033
Tides	2718	Tungusic language	4775	Vegetarianism	3240
Tiles	3875	Tunnels	3541	Velocipedes	4533
Timber	3609	Turkey, geography	2057	Venereal diseases	3280
Tin manufacture	3813	history	2056	Venezuela	2310
metallurgy	3816	travels	2057	Venice	2025–6
mining	3810	Turkey in Asia	2105	Ventilation	3914
Tithes	922	Turkish baths	3246	Ventriloquism	4592
Titles of honor	1833	language	4986–95	Vermont	2352
Tobacco	4040	literature	4649	Versification	5538
Toilet, toilet arts	4255	Turkistan	2115	Vertebrates (paleontology)	2734
Toleration	613	Turning	3911	(zoology)	2928
Tolls	1633	Tuscany	2025–6	Veterinary medicine	4142
Tombs	1840	Type-founding	3917	Villas	3582
Topographical engineering	3543	Typography	3917	Vine culture	4035
Total abstinence	1290, 3242	Tyrol	2035–6	Violin	4477–8
Toxicology	3522			Virginia	2365
Tractarianism	633	Understanding	1224	Virtue	1286
Tract societies	938	Uniforms	3715	Visible speech	5544
Trade	1628–1750	Unitarians	644	Vision (medically)	3275
Trade marks	1355	United States	2328–2440	(optically)	2633
Trades, mechanic	3801–4022	antiquities	1773	Visions and dreams	1282
unions	1472	directories	2344	Vital principle	3217
Tragedies, see Drama.		fine arts	4394	Vocal culture	4474
Transactions of societies, see names of subjects.		gazetteers	2343	music	4473–4
		geography	2341	organs	3217
Transcendentalism	1118	government	2337, 1831	". diseases of	3276
Translation	4621	history	2328–2440	Voice	3217
Transportation	1633	literature	4653	Volcanoes	2717
Transubstantiation	619	poetry	5566–7	Voyages, general	1761–2
Transylvania	2035–6	public documents	2339	round the world	1757
Trapping	4544	travels	2342	scientific	1758
Travels, collections of	1761	Universal geography	1753		
general	1762	history	1768	Wages	1470
scientific	1758	language	5531	Wakefulness	3239
Travelers, lives of	2541–2	Universalism	645	Waldenses	625
manuals for	1764	Universities	1509, 1592	Wales	2007

language	4955–64	Western Islands (Azores)	2251	Wool manufactures	3879
literature	4659	Western States	2348	Working classes	1470–3
music	4466	Western Territories	2349	Works, complete	5738
poetry	5575	Whale	2920	World, voyages round	1757
Walks	4533	Whale fisheries	3922	Worship	925–6, 961–4
Wallachia	2056–7	Wheat	4040	Wrecking and life saving	3758
Wallachian language	5231	Whigs, in U. S.	2887	Wrestling	4535
War, ethics	1459	English	1992–3	Writing (penmanship)	5540
" science and art	3713–51	Whist	4549	short-hand	5541–2
War of 1812	2332	Will (metaphysics)	880, 1225		
Warehouses	1633	(testamentary)	1354	Yachting	4536
Warming	3914	Wind instruments 4479–80, 4481		Year books, scientific	2591
Washington City	2364	Window gardening	4032	statistical	1770
Washington Territory	2390	Wine, wine culture	4035	Yellow-fever	3273
Watch-making	3912	Wisconsin	2383	Young men, morals of	1293
Water	2630	Wit	1225	Young Men's Christian Associations	941
Water colors	4395	(comic books)			
Water cure	3380	5750, 5752–3, 5568		Young Men's Christian Unions	941
Water wheels	3609	Witchcraft	819		
Water works	3547	Wives	1292, 1439	Young women, morals of	1294
Watering-places	3381	Wolff's philosophy	1108	Yucatan	2304–5
Waterloo	2043	Woman, education	1511, 1513		
Wax flowers	4258	social condition of	1438	Zend, language	4738–42
Wealth	1470	suffrage	1398–9	Zend Avesta	717
Weather	2719	Women, diseases of	3278	Zodiac	2693
Weaving	3878	lives of	2543–4	Zoology	2821–3000
Wedding customs	1839	morals for young	1294	Zoophytes	2936
Weights and measures	1690	Women's rights	1438	Zoroaster	717
Welsh, see Wales	3922	Wood engraving	4409	Zulus	2241
West Indies	2800–3	manufactures of	3922		
West Virginia	2392	Wool raising	4146		

BIBLIOLIFE

Old Books Deserve a New Life
www.bibliolife.com

Did you know that you can get most of our titles in our trademark **EasyScript**™ print format? **EasyScript**™ provides readers with a larger than average typeface, for a reading experience that's easier on the eyes.

Did you know that we have an ever-growing collection of books in many languages?

Order online:
www.bibliolife.com/store

Or to exclusively browse our **EasyScript**™ collection:
www.bibliogrande.com

At BiblioLife, we aim to make knowledge more accessible by making thousands of titles available to you – quickly and affordably.

Contact us:
BiblioLife
PO Box 21206
Charleston, SC 29413

Printed in Great Britain
by Amazon